The
MULLIGAN
JOURNAL

DAILY INSIGHTS
FROM THE OLD PRO

Produced with the assistance of Legacy, LLC.

www.Legacy-Management.com

Cover and interior designed by Larry Taylor Design, Ltd.

Cover photo: Romolo Tavani/iStock

Printed in the United States of America

www.MulliganClub.org

TABLE OF CONTENTS

FOREWORD

Friends,

It is such a blessing to have an Old Pro in our lives—someone who can love us, mentor us, and give us guidance and strength to live as we were designed to live. It was my great privilege to play such a wonderful character in *The Mulligan* movie.

In my role as an 87-year-old golf professional from Scotland, I met and mentored a young corporate man, Paul McAllister, who desperately needed a second chance in life. From the first moments I met him, I could tell he had achieved great success in life but fell far short of significance in the things that really counted: his relationships with his wife, his son, and many others around him.

One of the initial ways I was able to mentor this hotshot businessman was in offering him a personal journal. I asked him to evaluate the game of life each day and write down his good shots in one column and his mulligans in another. This journal became a powerful tool for Paul to evaluate his progress and growth as he learned to receive God's forgiveness and see life in a new light through the insights the Old Pro gave him during their lessons.

It is my prayer that you will use the journal you have in your hands in the same manner—that each day you will discover more of God's love for you and the unlimited forgiveness, grace, freedom, and purpose he offers you. I pray you will join me and thousands of other golfers and non-golfers from around the world in experiencing his wonderful gift of grace and, through the Ultimate Mulligan he offers, an eternal relationship you will forever enjoy.

Life is a special occasion. Don't miss it!

Pat Boone
The Old Pro

INTRODUCTION

God has a very clear purpose for your life—for you to walk with him in a close relationship. And he makes that relationship possible by giving you and everyone else who comes to him a second chance.

The purpose of *The Mulligan*—the book and the movie—is to illustrate that very simple reality. This unique journal you are holding is a practical means to walk out that reality daily. This book welcomes you into the beginning (or a re-beginning) of a beautiful, challenging, exciting adventure.

As you probably know, this new life is pictured in *The Mulligan* in golf terms. You are playing "the course less played" (life God's way) and being led by the perfect Caddy (Jesus), who knows you and the course intimately. The course comes with a guidebook (the Bible), which gives you all the information you need to play it well.

When you get to the end of life's course, you will need to turn in a perfect score-card—a scary prospect, considering none of us have one—but Jesus earned a perfect score and, amazingly, gives you his card to turn in as your own. That's wonderful news, whether you have never considered believing in Jesus before or have been caught up in religious demands you can never live up to. His perfection, not ours, is what gets us into heaven when our playing days are done. It also allows us to live with freedom and purpose today.

The Story of Paul McAllister

The Mulligan tells the story of a successful business executive named Paul McAllister, who discovers that he hasn't been very successful at life—or even at golf. After breaking his putter in a fit of anger in a Pro-Am, his golf professional tells him he's "not that good to get that bad" and sends him to his mentor Will Dunn—the Old Pro. Will and Paul develop a growing relationship, and during an early visit, the Old Pro hands Paul a personal journal, encouraging him to reflect on each day and write out his life's solid shots and mulligans. Paul begins to recognize his misplaced priorities and how they have damaged his relationships. He learns about how mulligans apply to life, and by receiving the Ultimate Mulligan that God offers everyone, he discovers his real purpose and starts down a new path and a new life.

Paul explains the turning point in his story well in his journal when he first lists his "solid shots" and "mulligans" (as you'll do in this journal).

> While we talked at lunch and afterward, the Old Pro explained the whole
> "Ultimate Mulligan" thing. I really listened. I think I have the basic concept.
> I feel good about my ability to grasp what he was talking about. It all sounds
> a bit religious to me, but I appreciate that Will is sincere about his faith.

In some ways, the idea of the Ultimate Mulligan and having a life-caddy who is better than the Old Pro seems too good to be true. What if I could have a perfect score?

Here is what I gleaned from Will's insights on playing the perfect round and getting the Ultimate Mulligan:

- We all fall short of a hundred; only God is perfect.
- God requires a perfect round, and we all fall short of that score.
- He sent his Son Jesus to play the perfect round for us — eighteen birdies.
- Jesus died on the cross for everyone, paid the penalty, and was resurrected. In essence, Jesus signed the card. All we have to do is attest to it and we get to turn it in as our own perfect round. That gives us a place in heaven and a lifetime caddy. That's what grace and forgiveness are all about.
- God's Ultimate Mulligan is ours through a friendship with Jesus. He gives us second chances every day, from the first tee to the last hole.
- God's course is not designed for the weak. One of the toughest tests of self-esteem is to bow your head and admit to the Lord you can't handle everything by yourself.
- Jesus wants to be my caddy and can help me play the game of life. Just as in golf, life was not meant to be played alone.

Prioritize the Relationship [1]

In a sense, Paul's story is everyone's story. The details are different for all of us, but misplaced priorities and broken relationships are common human experiences. Like Paul, we need the wisdom of an Old Pro to help us get back on the right path. We need to recognize what really matters and connect with the one who gave us life to begin with.

This is not about religion. Practicing a religion and trying to understand all its doctrines can get pretty complicated, and it usually leaves people feeling as if they are constantly falling short. This new life is about a relationship with our Caddy, Jesus. When we simply walk with him daily, we can go ahead and acknowledge that we've fallen short—no surprise there—and receive his forgiveness. Then we can "swing freely" in life, not stress about making par, enjoy the game, and become a lot better at it in the process.

This is a whole new way of looking at life, and golf provides us some wonderful illustrations to help us see it more clearly. You will find many of them in the pages that follow.

Establish Your Daily Practice

Like the Old Pro, we recommend entering your day slowly—taking some time to prepare for the day, prioritizing your relationships over your tasks, and asking God for his help. You are playing with Jesus as your Caddy, Brother, and Friend. It's best to begin each day in conversation with him. This journal is part of that conversation.

Starting your day slowly involves finding a place where you can consistently and quietly sit and listen without being tempted to get busy with your day. Just take some time to talk to God through prayer and let yourself become aware that Jesus is right there with you. Open your life up to him. Share what's on your heart and ask him what's on his. Embrace the mulligans he gives you every day as well as his promise to stand beside you and never leave you. Envision how your day with him will go and resolve to let him take the lead.

Something that can make this connection much easier is to pull up a chair and imagine Jesus sitting in it as the real person he is. You may even want to imagine him as a modern person you would feel comfortable talking to in everyday language. Then listen quietly and make some notes during the week about the encouraging words you hear. (If they are not encouraging, they are not from him; even when he corrects, he does it encouragingly.) This may seem awkward at first, perhaps even irreverent, but the point is to understand that he is approachable. He is the King of the universe, but he is also your Friend.

Remember what the Old Pro says: this new life is not about deeds but about believing and faith. You'll do a lot of good works, but you don't earn anything in this new life. It's all a gift. Live with gratitude and let yourself experience life to the fullest, the way the course designer intended.

How to Use this Journal

This interactive journal is an introduction to the wisdom and guidance of the course designer, who wants to partner with you as you play. You'll see many parallels between golf and life in the pages of this book, and if you take them to heart, your life—and your game—will be transformed.

There are 52 sections—you can do one a week if you like, but you don't have to follow a certain pace—and each section follows a similar structure. Page 1 leads off with a full-length reading that presents the theme for the section. It includes a Bible verse for you to reflect on, and having a Bible with you to look up the context or explore other verses is always a good idea. If you have a copy of *The Mulligan* book, keeping it nearby to refer to may be helpful for the following days too.

The next two pages offer some reflection questions and a noteworthy quote and provide space for recording your thoughts. Use these prompts as starting points for your journaling, not simply as questions that need to be answered concisely. The goal is not to get through a checklist but to spend time with God.

At the back of this book, you will see a table where you can list your "solid shots" and "need a mulligan" moments—the things you did well that week and things you wish you had done differently. Turn back to this section as often as needed as you go through the journal, listing the things you've done well and the areas where you'd like a do-over, and pray through your lists each week. Remember that these "mulligans" are not for beating yourself up but for recognizing where you may need to ask for forgiveness and for God's help in making up for them.

You will also see a prayer list at the end of the book. As you go through the journal, you will likely think about relationships in which you want to see reconciliation or restoration or receive God's direction. The prayer list provides a place to write dates when you first have these conversations with God and when any of these requests are answered. This is a great way to record his faithfulness and come back later to see how he has worked in your life.

The readings follow a general direction, beginning with life's big-picture issues, then God's answer to our greatest questions and needs, how life is all about relationships, how we develop a relationship with God, how we live out that relationship in the many areas of our lives, and finally how we pass on what we have learned to others. You'll notice that some themes come up more than once—that's by design—and some serve merely as starting points for directions you will want to follow throughout your life.

It is very important to remember that this book is not a collection of assignments to get through. As you follow Jesus, some of the verses and biblical principles here and the thoughts you have in response to them will become part of your daily conversation with him. Look at these insights simply as a conversation prompt—a companion guide to your daily walk with your Caddy and Friend. We trust that by the end, you will be able to look back to the beginning and see how much you've grown.

That's our prayer for you—that you will grow deeper in your relationship with Jesus, step further into his purposes for your life, and pick up some good golf tips along the way. You are like a club in his hands, and when you yield yourself to him, you will experience many beautiful swings and trajectories in your life. He is excited about walking with you on "the course less played"—life the way he meant it to be lived, full of love and joy in the adventure. And he is waiting at the first tee, ready for you to take the next step with him.

Play well and enjoy your round!

> Wally Armstrong
> Ken Blanchard
> Chris Tiegreen

[1] Ken Blanchard and Wally Armstrong, *The Mulligan* (Grand Rapids: Zondervan, 2010), 105-107.

The Mulligan Metaphor

THE ULTIMATE MULLIGAN

The Mulligan is a parable of second chances. If you're like most people, you've probably realized you need one. So imagine sitting down with the Old Pro over a cup of coffee and receiving his wisdom on golf, life, and faith. Listen as he shares some simple steps for receiving the Ultimate Mulligan.

THE OFFER

God has designed you to play his course—the course less played—with him by your side. Maybe you've based your self-worth on others' opinions or on your own performance in the past, but that's not what he wants for you. No, your self-worth is not up for grabs. He is the only one qualified to define who you are and lead you into a fulfilling way of life—not a life built on religion but based only on a relationship with him as your Friend. Jesus is your Caddy, and he wants you to walk with him in a new way, depending entirely on his love and forgiveness.

THE DILEMMA

God did not create you to be a robot. Out of his love, he gave you a choice—a way to have eternal life and friendship with him forever. We will all have to face God someday and turn in a perfect scorecard—a perfect life. But your scorecard isn't perfect, is it? Only one person in history has turned in a perfect scorecard. Our imperfections mean we will not make the cut and will be lost forever. As the Bible says, "For all have sinned and fall short of the glory of God" (Romans 3:23). We need a solution.

THE SOLUTION

God knows about your imperfect life. He knows you've fallen short of the requirements to enter heaven. You need a mulligan—a do-over you could never earn and that you don't deserve. So God sent his Son, Jesus, to play the perfect round and then offer you his scorecard as a gift. That's the Ultimate Mulligan. The Bible says, "For it is by grace you have been saved, through faith—and this is not from yourselves, it is the gift of

God" (Ephesians 2:8). There's only one way to receive this gift of a perfect scorecard: by choosing to accept God's offer of eternal life. If you do, you can stand before God one day and turn in Jesus' perfect round as your own.

THE DECISION
You can accept God's offer and gain eternal life by talking to him and acknowledging your need for forgiveness. Simply confess that you can't play life's perfect round. Ask for his forgiveness and decide to walk in a new direction. Let him know you're ready to play his course, not yours. The toughest test of self-esteem is bowing your head and saying this simple prayer of faith.

If you'd like to make that decision, here's a prayer you can use. Remember, it's not the exact words of the prayer but the attitude of your heart that counts.

"Dear God, I know I can't live a perfect life. I need the Ultimate Mulligan—Your forgiveness for my sins. Thank You for sending Your Son, Jesus, to live a perfect life and give me his perfect scorecard. From now on, I am ready to move in a new direction with Jesus by my side. I'm ready to play Your course and not mine. Thank You, Jesus, for dying for me. Please make me into the new person You want me to be. Amen."

THE NEW LIFE
If you prayed this prayer, Jesus is standing on the first tee to pick up your baggage—all of your sins, doubts, worries, and shame. He will put it on his back and walk with you as your Caddy and Friend for the rest of your life and on into eternity.

Jesus offers you unlimited mulligans, grace, and forgiveness. He wants you to start each day with him, walk with him throughout the day, and finish the day with him by your side. When that happens, you will experience the new life he offers and gain a whole new perspective on life.

If you made this decision or would like to get more information on what the Ultimate Mulligan is all about or what it means to walk with God as your Friend and Companion, please visit the Mulligan website at www.MulliganClub.org.

Seek first his kingdom
and his righteousness,
and all these things
will be given to you
as well.

MATTHEW 6:33

1
GOLF:
THE GAME OF LIFE FIRST

Golf and life have a lot in common. Both demand that we make numerous decisions, plan for a variety of hazards, manage our expectations, keep a balanced perspective, deal with disappointment, and proceed with confidence and hope. In fact, what we do on the course often reflects how we live our lives—the kind of person we are, the decisions we make, the priorities we have, how we respond to challenges, and how we handle success and failure. Over an eighteen-hole round, our personality, gifts, and temperament all rise to the surface. The course forces us to look in the mirror. It can serve as a very revealing picture of what's going on inside.

A lot of people don't make that connection. They think what happens on the course is simply a reflection of their game, so they prioritize their game to get better. They don't recognize how their play is exposing their insecurities, fears, disappointments, and emotional needs. That may seem like a lot to read into a golf game, but it's true. There's no shortage of Paul McAllisters who think they are simply frustrated with a sport and compensate by beating themselves up and resolving to do better. The game provides a barometer of their lives, and they misread it.

There's a simple way to avoid this problem: prioritize life over golf. In fact, Jesus teaches us to prioritize life over *everything*—or, more specifically, to prioritize God's will for our lives over all other agendas and interests. When we put the game of life first, everything else begins to fall into place. God begins to heal those insecurities, fears, and disappointments. We begin to see from a different perspective. And both life and golf become much more enjoyable and fulfilling.

Q: What do you enjoy most about golf? What are your true priorities when you hit the course? What is it about the game that draws you to it? Now ask the same question about life. What do you find meaningful and enjoy most about it? Do your focus and priorities line up with these values? In what ways have you already prioritized the game of life in your relationships, decisions, and lifestyle? In what ways do you think you might have gotten those priorities out of order?

"As you walk down the fairway of life you must smell the roses,
for you only get to play one round."
—Ben Hogan

*When I consider your
heavens, the work of your
fingers, the moon and the stars,
which you have set in place,
what is mankind that you are
mindful of them, human beings
that you care for them?*

PSALM 8:3-4

2

Life's Biggest Questions

Mastering the game of golf is a lifelong challenge guaranteed never to be completed. As soon as we think we have a handle on one part of our game, another seems to fall apart. Sometimes we come to the course full of confidence and leave with more questions than answers.

Life is full of questions too, and some of them are as big as questions can get. *Where did I come from? Who am I? Is there a God? If so, what is he like? What is the meaning of life, and what happens when I die?* We wonder about why we're here and where we're going, and if there's any more to life than making a name for ourselves or having as much fun as we can. If we don't know the answers to those big questions, we eventually end up wandering, searching, desperately hoping for something more, or even just filling up our lives so we don't have to think about the questions too much. We want to know if we're living for a purpose bigger than ourselves.

The good news is that we are. We were created with a specific design and called to fulfill a specific purpose. It's a wonderful plan, but there's a huge problem: we have all departed from our design and fallen short of our purpose. If that seems catastrophic, you're right. It is. It's humanity's greatest predicament. But that doesn't mean it's a hopeless situation.

Sometimes it seems hopeless. History is filled with stories of selfishness, greed, tyranny, war, bloodshed, pain, and suffering. But it's also lined with a greater story of hope, redemption, and restoration. Your longings are true, and your purpose is there to discover. The God who holds all answers is inviting you into them even now.

Q: In one way or another, every human being is in search of answers to life's biggest questions. To what degree have you been aware of that search in your own life? What are some of the questions you have asked about meaning and purpose? Have you looked for God and his answers as part of your search for meaning and purpose? If so, in what ways?

"Golf is deceptively simple and endlessly complicated;
it satisfies the soul and frustrates the intellect. It is at the same time
rewarding and maddening—and it is without a doubt the greatest game
mankind has ever invented."
—Arnold Palmer

*"What good is it
for someone to
gain the whole world,
yet forfeit their soul?"*

MARK 8:36

3
OUR EMPTY EFFORTS

Whether you are conscious of it or not, you have been on a spiritual journey looking for the answers to life's biggest questions. Many people are very aware of that journey; others keep pushing it aside, trying to prove their own significance while avoiding the question of why their significance even matters. Like a results-driven, Type-A executive who neglects his relationships for the bottom line or the next big acquisition—or even just a busy person with a long to-do list—we often let daily demands crowd out the meaning behind them all. Life can become one task after another.

Paul McAllister thought his real success had to do with the wealth he accumulated, the recognition he received, and the status that came with his accomplishments. Yet he still felt that something was missing. It's a common experience. Many of us look back over the years and wonder, *Is this what it's all about?* The answer, of course, is that life is about so much more than the momentary highs of temporary successes. And many of the people in our lives—often the casualties of our misplaced priorities—could probably point that out for us. There are heavy consequences for measuring success the wrong way.

The big questions create a void, and we have all kinds of ways of trying to fill it up. But none of our human efforts can fix the problems, answer the questions, or satisfy our deepest longings. Our seemingly unending mission to create meaning in our lives can only end when we realize it's headed in the wrong direction—when we finally leave behind the idea of getting ahead. Only then do our hearts open up to the answers God wants to give.

Q: Paul McAllister's life when he first met the Old Pro suggested that he had a distorted sense of priorities. What would you say are the top priorities in your life? What measurements would you use to determine whether you are successful in life? What are some of the consequences of measuring success the wrong way? Have you seen any of those consequences at work in your life? If so, how?

"Life in the presence of God should be known to us in conscious experience. It is a life to be enjoyed every moment of every day."
—A. W. Tozer

"*Come to me,*
all you who are weary
and burdened,
and I will give you rest."

MATTHEW 11:28

4
THE GAME INSIDE

The game of golf has a way of mirroring events that occur in real life. In golf as in life, focusing on impressing others can result in some embarrassing moments. In both golf and life, trying to compensate for insecurities by demanding perfection from yourself leads to a frustrating experience and missed opportunities to enjoy the people and world around you. In golf and life, beating yourself up for mistakes creates a horrible narrative in your own mind that leads to bad decisions, low expectations, and a poor self-image. In many ways, the "game" reveals a lot about what's going on inside.

In every area of life, whether at home, on the job, or at the course, we have to learn to deal with disappointments, adversity, and failures. One reason so many people are driven to succeed or obsessed about other people's opinions is that they are carrying deep wounds from past traumas—a parent or spouse who abandoned them, a friend who betrayed them, a respected authority figure who couldn't live up to their image. The world is full of hurting people trying to heal their own wounds with all kinds of coping strategies and wounding those around them in the process. Unfortunately, those strategies often lead us away from the Healer rather than toward him.

Do you recognize any of the symptoms of a wounded soul in yourself? They may have appeared in words that came out the wrong way, a volatile reaction to a minor frustration, or a slammed club or choice language on the golf course. Wherever they appear, don't beat yourself up for them. Take them as important signs that you are searching for relief, meaning, and answers. If you let them, they will lead you to a place of healing and hope.

Q: What is the narrative that goes through your mind when you make a bad mistake on the golf course? What do you say to yourself? Do you hear the same words when you make a mistake in life? How do you think that self-talk affects your thoughts, decisions, and relationships?

"Golf is the closest game to the game we call life.
You get bad breaks from good shots, and you get good breaks from bad
shots—but you have to play the ball where it lies."
—Bobby Jones

Jesus answered, "I am the way and the truth and the life. No one comes to the Father except through me."

JOHN 14:6

5
LIFE'S GREATEST ANSWER

To put it in golf terms, our greatest problem in life is the gap between the way God's course was meant to be played and the way we actually play it. That gap represents two hard realities: (1) We are required to sign a perfect scorecard at the end of God's course in order to be accepted by him; and (2) none of us has a perfect scorecard.

There is one exception, though. Jesus earned a perfect scorecard, and the good news is that God offers it to anyone who will receive it in place of their own. That requires some humility—most of us don't want to admit how bad our scorecard looks—but it's always a good trade. When we tear ours up by faith and accept his instead, we immediately get to have a relationship with God. At the end of life's round, we can turn in Jesus' perfect scorecard as if we had accomplished it ourselves and enjoy eternal life with him.

Knowing God through Christ is the answer to life's greatest questions. Jesus is the way, the truth, and the life—the *way* to become a child of God and live as he designed us to live, the *truth* about who God is and who we are, and the *life* that changes us from the inside out. In other words, he is everything we need, the key to finding our purpose and being fulfilled in it. Through him, we see the nature of God, we understand why we were created, we're empowered to live as we were designed to live, and we discover our eternal destiny. He brings an end to our wandering, searching, and avoiding the big questions. He turns our frustrating game of life into the most satisfying round we've ever played.

Q: Do you feel as if you've been trying to earn a perfect scorecard in life? If so, what has that experience been like? How successful do you think you've been? What are the implications of Jesus' gift of a perfect scorecard? How do you think it might change the way you approach your life?

"This is and has been the Father's work from the beginning—
to bring us into the home of his heart."
—George MacDonald

In him we have redemption
through his blood,
the forgiveness of sins,
in accordance with the riches
of God's grace
that he lavished on us.

EPHESIANS 1:7-8

6
THE ULTIMATE MULLIGAN

As a golfer, you know all about mulligans. Playing partners have probably offered them to you many times. You've probably offered them to your partners many times too. Or maybe you're like Paul McAllister, who played strictly by the rules and was too proud to receive "charity" for a bad shot. In either case, you learned early on about this expression of grace and, whether you received it or not, how often it is needed.

God and mulligans go together. He came up with the idea of second chances, and third and hundredth chances too. In fact, he offers us the Ultimate Mulligan—a one-time gift that we could never earn on our own that covers the entire round of our lives. He offers plenty of daily mulligans too to cover all the bad shots we will ever make. These mulligans can't be earned; that's the whole point of a mulligan in the first place. It has to be offered by a playing partner and received as a gift. But once we receive the Ultimate Mulligan from God, our entire game changes.

The Ultimate Mulligan is not a "what" but a "who." Jesus earned the perfect scorecard and makes up for all the bad shots we will ever make. He compensates for our imperfections and provides for all we lack. He forgives us of our sins, helps us learn from our mistakes, and walks with us as we play his course. He is very patient; he understands that our shots sometimes veer off into the woods or find the bottom of a lake. But he is the ultimate playing partner too. We can trust that he will always guide us back into the fairways and onto the open greens of life.

Q: Since perfection is the only way to gain eternal life, we have only two options: to be perfect (which we've already failed at doing) or to receive someone else's perfect record in our place. It should be obvious which one of those applies to each of us, but many people live as though they are still trying for the impossible goal. Why do you think that is? What are some common barriers to accepting the Ultimate Mulligan? How easily do you accept mulligans—offers of forgiveness—from God and other people?

"Forget the last shot.
It takes so long to accept that you can't always replicate your swing.
The only thing you can control is your attitude toward the next shot."
—Mark McCumber

*It is by grace you have been
saved, through faith—
and this is not from yourselves,
it is the gift of God—
not by works,
so that no one can boast.*

EPHESIANS 2:8-9

7
WHO DO YOU THINK YOU ARE?

Whatever Paul McAllister achieved, it was never enough. He was successful at many things, but his heart was always unsettled. The accolades and achievements never fully satisfied him, so the job was never done. If he had recognized how unquenchable his thirst for fulfillment was, he might have slowed down to find out why. He might have recognized that his life had been an unending, futile mission to fill that void. But he was too busy, always looking for the next thing—the next mountain to climb, the next business to acquire, even just a single-digit handicap.

What was Paul's problem? Like all human beings, he had experienced heartaches and disappointments earlier in life that left him feeling empty. He tried to fill that emptiness by basing his identity on his performance. It's a common tendency, but it never works because performance is never absolute. It keeps changing. There's always more to accomplish and always the possibility of falling short. Our own performance can only satisfy us for a moment before we start to feel empty again.

The root of this problem is self-perception—how we see ourselves when we look in the mirror. If we don't recognize who we are, how God made us, and how he sees us, we spend our lives trying to become "somebody." When we base our identity on our performance, we tend to expect perfection and end up disappointed. But when we realize that we are already "somebody" in God's eyes—a person made in his image whom he thoroughly loves—we are set free. We may *want* to perform well, but we don't *have to* in order to prove our worth. Like golfers who play simply for the joy of the game, we are free to live without the pressure of proving who we are.

Q: It is often said that when we base our identity on our performance, we become "human doings" rather than human beings. Can you relate to this dynamic? In what ways have you tried to become "somebody" through the things you accomplish or the people you know?

"Aren't you, like me, hoping some person, thing, or event will come along
to give you that final feeling of inner well-being you desire?
Don't you often hope, *May this book, idea, course, trip, job, country,
or relationship fulfill my deepest desire*?
But as long as you are waiting for that mysterious moment,
you will go on running helter-skelter, always anxious and restless,
always lustful and angry, never fully satisfied.
You know that this is the compulsiveness that keeps us going and busy,
but at the same time makes us wonder whether we are getting anywhere
in the long run. This is the way to spiritual exhaustion and burnout.
This is the way to spiritual death.
Well, you and I don't have to kill ourselves. We are the Beloved."
—Henri Nouwen

The Lord your God is with you,
the Mighty Warrior who saves.
He will take great delight in you;
in his love he will no longer
rebuke you, but will rejoice
over you with singing.

ZEPHANIAH 3:17

8
WHO DO YOU
THINK GOD IS?

"The God I worship is a loving God," said the Old Pro. "I don't think he made any junk." Even though many people would agree with that statement, most of us tend to think about ourselves negatively, and sometimes we assume God does too. Perhaps he loves us like a harsh disciplinarian loves his trainees, or maybe he's more like a disappointed parent loving a problem child. We often define ourselves by our mistakes and then beat ourselves up for them. We end up living under an impossible standard.

It's true that God's standards are extremely high, but he also knows we are not capable of living up to them and provides a way for us to receive Jesus' scorecard in place of our own. The reason he made us in his image was for us to be able to relate to him in love. If we're ever going to experience his love, we have to understand that he loves us because he wants to, not because he has to. He places an enormous value on our lives.

When we think our value in God's eyes is up for grabs, we live under the weight of constant pressure and impossible expectations. But when we realize our self-worth is securely anchored in his love, we can relax. Yes, we still make mistakes at times, but he offers us more mulligans than we could ever need. We can try to correct our mistakes and change our behavior without feeling the weight of guilt and shame. We put the rat-race for results behind us. We can endure the ups and downs of the game of life because we have the unshakeable assurance that we are loved, forgiven, and accepted in his eyes.

Q: How do you think God sees you? How does that perception affect the way you think and live? How does the understanding that God highly values you and will not change his love for you resolve any insecurities, anxieties, and need to prove yourself?

"What comes into our minds when we think about God
is the most important thing about us."
—A.W. Tozer

Anyone who comes to him must believe that he exists and that he rewards those who earnestly seek him.

HEBREWS 11:6

9

THE HAZARD OF
MISPERCEPTIONS

Have you ever played a hole—or even an entire course—that made you wonder what the course designer was thinking? Small greens, huge hazards, narrow fairways, and unreasonable slopes sometimes turn the game into an impossible challenge, especially when you're already having a bad day. You might start to think the architect was trying to weed out all but the best golfers. It can feel personal.

It isn't, obviously. You might play the same course the next week and enjoy the challenge. But when you're battling through adversity, your perspective gets skewed. You start to think that maybe golf is a sadistic game, or you'll never be as good as you want to be. And it's an easy step from there to resenting the fact that you can't ever seem to enjoy yourself.

That's a taste of how many people feel when they think about God. Religion and experience have often portrayed him the wrong way. People wonder why so many people suffer, assume God doesn't care, and have been taught that he is holding all their sins against them. All the distorted images and unanswered questions make them doubt whether he exists, or to want nothing to do with him if he does.

Misperceptions about God are a complicated hazard to get out of, but there is a way out. You begin to discover and appreciate who he really is by encountering someone who reflects his nature, immersing yourself in truth as expressed in God's Word, the Bible, and letting him reorient your vision. That's much of what this journal is about, but it's only a step in a long-term process of getting to know him. As you do, you find that he is full of love, happy to show it to you, and far better than anyone could imagine.

Q: Misperceptions of God take many forms—an absentee landlord, a detached observer, a demanding parent, a strict disciplinarian looking for opportunities to correct us, a heavenly Santa Claus who could just give us whatever we want if he's real, among others. Which images of him do you tend to think of most? Have you ever tried to hide your real self from God? How does an accurate perception of God make that effort not only impossible but unnecessary?

"God loves you more than you'll ever know. Not your image,
not your happy face, not your spirituality—but you. The real you.
The one you think nobody knows about. No, real love is *not* blind.
Because his eyes are always open, he can see what you cannot.
And he felt that what he saw in you was worth dying for."
—Bingham Hunter

"God opposes the proud but shows favor to the humble."
Humble yourselves, therefore, under God's mighty hand, that he may lift you up in due time.

1 PETER 5:5-6

10
THE HAZARD OF PRIDE

Imagine standing at the tee and looking down the fairway ahead. At about the distance of your normal drive, you see a hazard on the right and another on the left. Some fairways are set up to test your mettle, and this one is tempting you. Pride says to go for that narrow strip of grass lined with danger, while wisdom urges a shorter drive. You have a critical decision to make.

Understanding your true identity is like that fairway. Danger lies on each side of it. On one side, there's the false humility of a negative self-image, of kicking yourself for every mistake and demanding a better performance next time. On the other is the pride of thinking you can handle things on your own, of refusing even the simple grace of a mulligan generously offered. How do you navigate that critical decision—a moment in golf, a constant dilemma in life? What can you do to avoid the hazards of false humility and pride?

Lay up. True humility embraces wisdom because it has no need to impress, no opinion other than God's to satisfy, no guilt or shame to compensate for. Neither false humility nor pride will ever accept the Ultimate Mulligan of Jesus or any of the daily mulligans he offers along the way. But genuine humility sees the end game and sacrifices a moment of glory for the ultimate prize. It allows you to embrace the amazing truth of who you are and how much you are loved without feeling entitled to it. It trains your eyes to see everything as a gift and enjoy the one who gives it. It enhances the joy of the game.

Q: In what ways, if any, have you seen unrealistic personal standards caused by pride and/or a negative self-image create undue stress and personal conflicts in your life?

"Golf is a game that is played on a five-inch course—
the distance between your ears."
—Bobby Jones

There is now no condemnation
for those who are in Christ Jesus,
because through Christ Jesus
the law of the Spirit
who gives life has set you free
from the law of
sin and death.

ROMANS 8:1-2

11
THE HAZARD OF PERFECTIONISM

The Old Pro had seen it many times before—a performance-driven player approaching golf and life with impossible expectations and brutal self-criticism for falling short of them. The joy of the game gets lost in that attitude. So do relationships. When people base their significance on achieving perfection—or even something close to it—everything else becomes a distraction. "If you want to be good at golf and life," he said, "you have to stop putting your self-worth up for grabs based on your performance or the opinion of others."

Perfectionism, performance, and people-pleasing are dangerous hazards. It's hard to play your way out of them. But you can avoid them by accepting the fact that God has already determined your self-worth, and it's completely secure. It has nothing to do with how well you perform or what people think of you. When you realize that, your sense of identity can endure all the ups and downs of good and bad days.

If your scoring system as a golfer is all about winning and others' opinions, you'll miss out on what the game is all about—having fun, building relationships, and enjoying the environment. The same is true for every other area of your life too. You were not designed for perfectionism—the unhealthy, obsessive pursuit of an impossible standard. God released you from that burden when he gave you Jesus' perfect scorecard. With that already in hand, you've got nothing left to add to it. Ironically, your performance will probably improve the less you focus on it. You can swing freely and live without pressure. You have nothing left to do but relax and enjoy the course.

Q: We all love and need affirmation, but we can't always depend on getting it from other people. Have you found yourself trying to perform well for the praise others might give you? Are you driven by a need for respect or human affirmation? If so, how does this put your self-esteem up for grabs? How does it turn golf and life into matters of achievement rather than matters of relationships?

"Nothing is lacking in our lives but our work to believe, in him and in his Word. You get there by believing things that seem too good to be true. And when you struggle, doubt, or are anxious, just ask yourself, *What am I not believing?*"
—Wally Armstrong

"Come, follow me."

MATTHEW 4:19

12
THE COURSE LESS PLAYED

God created us to play the course he designed the way he meant it to be played. It's a wonderful course—the most beautiful ever designed, the most "royal and ancient" of all—but it isn't easy. God eagerly invites us to play it according to his rules and in a relationship with him. Those are not burdensome terms, but the course seems intimidating to many, so it remains the course less played. Most people go play their own course their own way.

We have that choice. God gave us free will to play whichever course we desire. But as much as going off to play your own course seems like it would lead to freedom and happiness, it doesn't. It separates a person from God and eventually leads to frustration and futility. Though it's easier to play than God's course, it's much harder to enjoy.

No one but Jesus has played God's course the way it was meant to be played. He's the only person ever to make the cut. But because we are given his perfect scorecard, we no longer have to worry about playing a perfect round. We can simply enjoy being with God on his course and learning how to play his way. We want to do as well as we can, obviously; the better we do, the more we get out of the game. But we don't have to be afraid of missing the cut.

That's the offer before you and every other human being, and accepting it not just once but every single day will transform your life. The course less played includes much more than eternal life, as wonderful as that is. It involves a relationship with God, a new perspective on life, and joy in the journey. And it's an adventure every step of the way.

Q: Why do you think many people find it hard to play God's course by his rules in relationship with him? What is the appeal of going to play your own course your own way? In what ways have you experienced the futility and frustration of playing your own course your way?

"We are always in the presence of God. . . .
There is never a non-sacred moment! His presence never diminishes.
Our awareness of his presence may falter,
but the reality of his presence never changes."
—Max Lucado

*Do nothing out of selfish
ambition or vain conceit.
Rather, in humility value others
above yourselves,
not looking to your own interests
but each of you to the interests
of the others.*

PHILIPPIANS 2:3-4

13
It's All About Relationships

To play the course less played, you'll need to hold on to a very important truth: It's all about relationships. The skills and the scores of the game make for an interesting challenge, and the beauty of the environment makes for an enjoyable experience. But at the heart of this course's design is one overarching relationship and many others that fit into it.

People who have become human doings rather than human beings will have trouble with this until they make some major adjustments. There will be huge obstacles in the way: a performance mindset that focuses on tasks rather than people; a fear of getting hurt by investing too much in relationships; the pride of wanting to do things your own way for your own glory; a preoccupation with mistakes and failures that turns your attention inward; and many other insecurities and false assumptions that might redirect your energy away from the Creator of the course and the people you're playing with. You'll have to become vulnerable and learn to connect if you want to play the course well.

Learn to major on relationships. Reach out to people and let them reach out to you. It's true that some people are more social than others—you don't have to change your personality—but everyone needs a deep connection with God and strong friendships with others who know him. If you score well without enjoying fellowship along the way, you've missed the whole point. But if you prioritize the fellowship, you may see the "score" of your life improve and be able to relax when it doesn't. And the course less played will become a much more rewarding experience.

Q: Relationships are a key component in our lives that we often use, mis-use, or ignore. In what ways have you seen yourself doing this? What are some of your relationship tendencies that you would like to change?

"If there has come to us the miracle of friendship,
if there is a soul to which our soul has been drawn,
it is surely worthwhile being loyal and true."
—Hugh Black

"Now this is eternal life:
that they know you,
the only true God,
and Jesus Christ,
whom you have sent."

JOHN 17:3

14
THE MOST IMPORTANT RELATIONSHIP

Imagine being invited to an unfamiliar golf course and overhearing a conversation about the course's origins in the clubhouse. "The owner actually designed this course for his son," one golfer says. "He tailored it to his son's skills, lined the fairways with his son's favorite trees, and invited only his son's friends to play." You may wonder how you got an invitation to this exclusive place; did the person who invited you know that owner's son? In any case, you immediately feel privileged to be there. You also want to get to know this special golfer whose father gave such an extravagant gift.

That's the situation you find yourself in as a player on the course less played. The Creator of the universe designed this course for his Son, and only the Son's friends get to play it. In fact, the Son insists on playing it with his friends, as it was created for his pleasure and he doesn't like to play by himself. And since he knows every dip and swell of the terrain, the carry distance to every green from every spot on the course, every hazard to avoid and every trick for getting out of them when you happen to hit them anyway, the bend of the grass and swirl of the breeze at any time of day—in other words, there isn't a detail about this course he doesn't know—you can't imagine a better partner. It would be a joy to play a round with this remarkable man.

Commit to approach your life as you would approach a course like that. If you don't yet know the Son, all it takes is a prayer asking to receive him into your life. Then embark on that journey. There is no better course than the one less played.

Q: Have you ever wished you had an insider's view of how life works—the best approaches, the knowledge of when to lay up and when to go for it, an assurance of how it's all going to work out? How would that insider's view change the way you live?

"Incredible as it may seem, God wants our companionship.
He wants to have us close to him. He wants to be a father to us, to shield us,
to protect us, to counsel us, and to guide us in our way through life."
—Billy Graham

Whether you turn to the right or to the left, your ears will hear a voice behind you, saying, "This is the way; walk in it."

ISAIAH 30:21

15
THE PERFECT CADDY

Playing the course less played—the one created for the Son and his friends—is going to be an exciting adventure. And as someone introduced to the Son, you're looking forward to spending time with him. But when you arrive at the first tee, you realize he's not just there to play. He is standing there like a caddy, ready to help you navigate your round with his wisdom and advice. This expert on the course who knows its every nuance and detail is going to coach you every step of the way.

That's what Jesus does in our lives, or rather what his Spirit does as we submit to him and listen. He is waiting on the first tee, ready to grab our bag and guide us. His course is now our course to enjoy. We have to stick the tee in the ground and make all the shots—he isn't going to take over and do it for us—but he will walk with us and be there for every one of them. He is available to talk it over and help us strategize.

Golf was originally meant to be played by a two-person team. A caddy knew his course and all his player's strengths, weaknesses, and distances. He would show the player where to aim, and the player had to trust him completely. A victory was credited to the team. The game was not meant to be played alone.

Life isn't meant to be lived alone either, and the perfect Caddy stands ready to guide you if you will trust him. You'll need to learn how to listen—more on that later—and you'll need to commit to following his advice. But whenever he is a member of a team, the result is always amazing.

Q: Some players listen to their caddy more than others. In *The Mulligan*, Paul McAllister thought he knew better than his caddy at the pro-am, even though he had never played the course before. Where do you think you fall on that spectrum—in golf and in life? Do you take advice well or tend to do things your own way? What are some examples of your approach?

"We are not alone on our journey. The God of love who gave us life
sent us [his] only Son to be with us at all times and in all places,
so that we never have to feel lost in our struggles but always
can trust that God walks with us."
—Henri Nouwen

Do not conform to the pattern
of this world,
but be transformed by the
renewing of your mind.

ROMANS 12:2

16
THE FIRST TEE SHOT

"Dad, how will this make a difference in your life?" Jake asked when Paul told him about his decision to accept Jesus and play the course less played. It's a legitimate question that much of the world is asking when they observe followers of Jesus. *Does following him really have practical implications? Can it salvage a broken relationship? Can he really change a life?* A lot of people say they believe in Jesus. Not as many demonstrate how their belief changes anything.

Saying yes to the Ultimate Mulligan is lifechanging, but the transformation doesn't happen all at once. Sometimes a new beginning is just taking the next step, making the next decision in a relationship, a work situation, a personal issue, or any other area of life. But that first step can have far-reaching implications. The gift of forgiveness and eternal life in Jesus begins to change us from the inside out and works its way outward in what we do, how we speak, and who we relate to. As we grow as Jesus' followers, people around us benefit.

As you play the course less played with Jesus as your Caddy, you'll notice some immediate changes as well as some that begin now and take a long time to develop. That's okay; be patient with the process. Let him rearrange your priorities, be willing to become more vulnerable and open in your relationships, ask for forgiveness from those you've wronged, and let reconciliation and healing begin. Demonstrate your changed heart wherever and whenever you can through your words, actions, and attitudes. And let those attitudes include the love and joy of a life set free. You will become a blessing to those around you and a powerful testimony of the Caddy's amazing grace.

Q: When you accept the Ultimate Mulligan, changes occur from the inside out and have a profound impact on your relationships. This involves asking for forgiveness for wrongs you've committed, offering forgiveness to others for their mistakes, and becoming vulnerable in reaching out and investing yourself in relationships. Do any of these changes seem challenging to you? If so, how? If you could restore or reconcile any relationship in your life, which one would you choose? What steps can you take today to start that process of reconciliation and restoration?

"Achievements on the golf course are not what matters;
decency and honesty are what matter."
—Tiger Woods

Rejoice always, pray continually,
give thanks in all circumstances;
for this is God's will for you
in Christ Jesus.

1 THESSALONIANS 5:16-18

17
CONVERSATIONS WITH GOD

Conversations between a player and caddy are a vital aspect of the game. They focus on strategy, club selection, course conditions, reading the greens, and more. A player could try to figure out everything on his own if he wanted to, but why not take advantage of the caddy's expertise? And considering the Caddy who walks through life with us, the expertise is immense. It's essential to stay in close contact with him on every shot we make.

That's what prayer is—having conversations with Jesus. A lot of people think of prayer as a skill or a discipline and want to know how to do it, but at its heart, it simply means talking with Jesus and his Father as friends. It's great to start that conversation in the morning, but it can continue throughout the day and night. If life is all about relationships and this is the most important one, then conversation with God is part of our design. It's one of the reasons he made us. He loves us and wants us to walk and talk with him always.

God is always available. He never runs out of time, never turns away no matter what you've done, and never gives up because it has been a long time since you last talked with him. He is the best Friend you could ever have and is perfectly comfortable with skipping the formalities and hearing what's on your heart. Whatever advice or help you need, prayer should always be a first response rather than a last resort. The more you talk with him, the closer your relationship gets, the more your perspective on life changes, and the better you get at playing the course less played.

Q: Have you, like Paul, ever found yourself thinking, *Why am I trying to figure this out by myself? Help is a prayer away.* If so, how did that experience play out? What did you ask, and how was it answered? Do you think God guides you even when you don't hear something specific from him?

"You need not cry very loud; he is nearer to us than we think."
—Brother Lawrence

"My sheep listen to my voice;
I know them,
and they follow me."

JOHN 10:27

18
THE VOICE OF YOUR BEST FRIEND

Prayer is a familiar concept, so not many people are surprised by the idea of talking to God, even if they aren't quite sure how to do it. But hearing God speak? That's another story. Many question whether it's possible. Even if they believe it is, they are very uncertain about what he might say and how they can know he said it.

The Bible assures us that we can hear God's voice. Jesus said he would continue to speak to his followers. He does that in many ways, and as the Old Pro says, we usually don't hear him with our ears. But we can still be confident that we've heard him. He is eager for us to understand his thoughts and learn his ways. He is not a silent Caddy.

One way we can hear from God is through his love letter, the Bible. Some call it Basic Instruction Before Leaving Earth, but it's also the designer's notes on the course less played. It has advice and instructions on all kinds of things, teaching us the art of living, telling us the stories of those who have gone before, and declaring rock-solid promises God wants us to believe. It isn't a chore to read his Word. It's how we get to know him and understand him.

We can also ask him in any situation to teach us and guide us. He wants to share his wisdom. When we get quiet and ask him a question, often our thoughts are redirected to ideas we had not yet considered. It may not happen in an instant, but he will find a way to open our minds and hearts to what he is saying. As we read his word and listen in our spirit, he teaches us what he wants us to know.

Q: The Old Pro told Paul that the Good Book tells us how the play the Game Of Life First the way the designer of the course meant for it to be played. In that sense, it is an instruction manual, but it is also more—a living conversation between God and us. How does God speak to us about specific situations in our lives through his Word? How are we more likely to hear from him if we are reading with the expectation that he will speak?

"So wait before the Lord. Wait in the stillness.
And in that stillness, assurance will come to you.
You will know that you are heard; you will know that your Lord ponders
the voice of your humble desires; you will hear quiet words spoken to you
yourself, perhaps to your grateful surprise and refreshment."
—Amy Carmichael

"*I no longer call you servants, because a servant does not know his master's business. Instead, I have called you friends, for everything that I learned from my Father I have made known to you.*"

JOHN 15:15

19
MORE THAN A CADDY

The player-caddy relationship in golf is more than a professional partnership. It often involves all the familiarity, trust, honesty, and reliability of a friendship. But it's still a friendship focused on strategizing and executing, and there are no guarantees of it lasting forever. In other words, it's for a season and mostly about "doing." A truer friendship goes deeper, reaches further into "being," and lasts. It involves every area of life.

That's why Jesus is more than a Caddy for us. He is also an intimate Friend. He does want to give us instructions and advice, but he also wants to hear about our insecurities, flaws, failures, regrets, fears, and disappointments—as well as all our hopes, dreams, and desires. It's a comprehensive relationship that never stops growing deeper.

You can tell Jesus anything because he saw something in you that was worth dying for. He is not interested in keeping a professional distance, maintaining decorum, or putting boundaries around the relationship. He wants to hear it all, from the big questions to the minor frustrations. He not only wants to show you how to play the course but to comfort you in times of need and stir up your faith in times of uncertainty. He is always ready for the next step in the relationship.

No matter how many close friends or confidants you have had before, this one is different. He already knows you more intimately than anyone else; he invites you to know him intimately too. As you get to know him, and if you let him, he can calm all your worries and fears, heal your regrets and disappointments, help you grow out of your insecurities, and fulfill the desires he has given you. He cares about it all—and promises to walk with you through it all.

Q: "Friendship is what love looks like when put into practice," the Old Pro said. "It's having someone who genuinely cares about you and hangs in there with you no matter what." This is the kind of friend Jesus wants to be for us. In what ways did the Old Pro demonstrate this quality of friendship? Is there anything you feel you can't talk to Jesus about? If so, what? Why do you think it is difficult to talk about it with him?

"Jesus said that he tells his friends all that his Father has told him;
close friends communicate thoroughly and make a transfer of heart
and thought. How awesome is our opportunity to be friends with God,
the almighty Creator of all!"
—Beverly LaHaye

If anyone is in Christ,
the new creation has come:
The old has gone,
the new is here!

2 CORINTHIANS 5:17

20
A Transforming Relationship

You've likely heard the expression of one person "rubbing off" on another. It suggests that simply by being around someone, we can pick up on that person's character, habits, or personality. Relationships are influential—we've all experienced being shaped in some degree by the people we spend time with. But some relationships are more influential than others, and sometimes the transformation is obvious.

Our friendship with Jesus is the most transformative relationship we can have. He is the source of genuine change in our lives, and he wants to influence us with everything that is good, true, and wonderful about his nature and his kingdom. He wants to "rub off" on us in ways that will give us a new life and a new perspective. That transformation begins when we first accept him as our Savior—what the Bible calls a new birth—but it is meant to continue throughout our lives. We become different simply by being with him and learning from him.

The more we spend time with him, then, the more we become like him. We grow into his image, which is the perfect image of God we were designed to carry from the beginning. As we walk with him, talk with him, learn from him, and grow through him, we come to look like the new creations we actually are. The truth about us becomes visible.

Your use of this devotional journal is a huge step in that direction. It's one way to spend time with Jesus and let him rub off on you. You are becoming like your Caddy and Friend. Make that a lifelong commitment, and you'll be amazed at the lifelong results.

Q: In what ways have you tried to change yourself in the past by learning new things, developing new habits, and applying willpower? How successful have those efforts been? Why do you think spending time with Jesus is the key to change? What happens when we talk with him throughout our day and take time to listen to him? Why is this more transforming than our efforts at changing ourselves?

"Holiness only appears to be abnormal.
The truth is, holiness is normal, and to be anything else is to be abnormal.
Being a saint is simply being the person God made me to be."
—James C. Howell

"*Everyone who hears these words of mine and puts them into practice is like a wise man who built his house on the rock.*"

MATTHEW 7:24

21
MANAGING YOUR PLAYING TIME

We live in a demanding world that pulls us in multiple directions. Things are added to our to-do list faster than we can check them off. Our various roles and the people around us compete for our attention. It takes a lot of dedication and commitment to fulfill our responsibilities, and even then we may feel like we're always a little behind and having to catch up. The "rat race" takes a hefty physical, emotional, and relational toll. We're reminded often that we can't do everything. We have to choose. And those choices always, in one way or another, reflect something about our priorities.

Making sure our highest priorities get the most attention is often a matter of time management. Managing time is not just a matter of better organizational skills that help us get more done. It's an opportunity to identify what's most important to us and how we can make sure it doesn't get squeezed out of our busy schedules. If a hectic schedule is harming our relationships, we are no longer managing time; it is managing us. We need to regain control.

This is a significant part of your transformation. There is always more to be done than you are humanly able to do, so you will have to sacrifice some things. What will they be? Before you answer that question, determine which aspects of your life are non-negotiable: things like time with Jesus, time with loved ones, physical and emotional health, and whatever you need (not want) to do to provide for yourself and your family. It's much easier to fit options around essentials than to try to fit essentials in around options. Remember that life is all about relationships. Make sure they aren't left out.

Q: Managing time is not just about better organization skills in order to accomplish more tasks. It is an invitation to identify what really is important in your life (which is why the Old Pro suggested renaming an alarm clock as an "opportunity clock"). How might this perspective change the way you approach your day? What would your schedule look like not as a have-to list but as a get-to list? In what ways does your time management reflect relationships as a priority?

"Your walk with God is essential.
His heart is not seen in an occasional chat or weekly visit.
We learn his will as we take up residence in his house
every single day."
—Max Lucado

In the morning, Lord,
you hear my voice;
in the morning
I lay my requests before you
and wait expectantly.

PSALM 5:3

22
ENTER YOUR DAY SLOWLY

"We have two selves," the Old Pro explained to Paul. "An inner self that is thoughtful, reflective, and a good listener; and an outer, task-oriented self that is focused on achieving and getting things done. The outer self is too busy to learn. And which of these two selves do you think wakes up quicker in the morning?" As you can probably guess, the task-oriented self usually takes over the morning and leads into the day. The thoughtful self gets pushed aside much too often.

That's why it's important to enter our days slowly. Just as we would warm up at the range before hitting a few balls and beginning a round of golf, we need to do some spiritual "stretching" to loosen up, talking with our Caddy and Friend before jumping into the day's schedule. Warming up mentally and emotionally prepares us to face the challenges that may come. And if it doesn't happen in the morning, it's likely not to happen at all. Good things come up that interfere with good intentions. It's important to protect that time.

In addition to the journaling you've been doing, a good way to spend that time is to envision walking through the day with your Caddy and Friend. Go ahead and talk about some of the things you expect to come up and how you should handle them. Ask him for his help in advance. Picture yourself at the end of the day thanking him for how well everything went as he walked by your side. You will begin to see your days with greater purpose and enter them with greater peace. And you'll be sure not to miss the company of your best Friend.

Q: "Few people ever wake up to their inner selves," the Old Pro said. "We don't even do it on vacation. We race around from one activity to another and then come home exhausted." Can you relate to this description? If so, what are some of the consequences of not being in touch with your inner self? What adjustments do you need to make, if any, to follow through on the commitment to start your day slowly?

"If we really believe not only that God exists
but also that he is actively present in our lives—
healing, teaching, guiding—
we need to set aside a time and space
to give him our undivided attention."
—Henri Nouwen

Do you not know that your bodies are temples of the Holy Spirit, who is in you, whom you have received from God? You are not your own; you were bought at a price. Therefore honor God with your bodies.

1 CORINTHIANS 6:19-20

23
TAKE CARE OF YOUR TEMPLE

Physical conditioning has a lot to do with how well we swing the club. We need muscle tone in our hands and forearms, leg strength for balance and leverage, and flexibility for a full rotation, among other things. It isn't hard to see some spiritual parallels—taking care of our inner self is a high priority—but it's important to take care of our outer self too. For golf and for the rest of life, our bodies are a valuable gift. We need to treat them well.

We have obvious self-interest in staying in shape. It helps us feel better and live longer. But there are greater reasons than our own benefit: We are a temple of the Lord, a place where his Spirit has chosen to dwell. When we receive Jesus as our Savior and walk with him as our Friend, we are born of God's Spirit and have new life. He comes to live inside of us. We become a sacred space for God's presence in this world.

That's why the Old Pro took a walk every morning as part of his routine for entering the day slowly, and why he was so committed to it rain or shine—that no-excuses, "no matter what" philosophy of people who live for a greater purpose than themselves. It's an important responsibility. As the Bible says, we are no longer our own. We are vessels used for the Lord's honor.

Take that responsibility seriously, both for your own health and for the work God wants to do through you. He has chosen you as a place of his presence so the world might experience something of his nature as he lives in you. Make the most of that opportunity. Condition yourself to last.

Q: "Committed people don't know about excuses," the Old Pro said. "They only know about results." When it's raining, they don't think, *I better stay inside today.* They think, *I'd better wear my rain gear.* In what areas of life do you have that "no matter what" philosophy? In what areas do you need to adopt it? How does being a temple of the Holy Spirit affect your self-perception? What implications does it have for what God wants to do in you and through you?

TAKE CARE OF YOUR TEMPLE

"There's no such thing as bad weather,
only inappropriate clothing!"
—Anonymous

"Surely
I am with you always,
to the very end of the age."

MATTHEW 28:20

24

Treasure Your Time with Jesus

Weeks ago, we imagined a fairway lined with hazards, a dangerous situation on both sides. It's a metaphor for many situations in life in which we must navigate between two extremes or avoid two pitfalls. One of those situations is the way we cultivate a relationship with Jesus. On one side, there's the temptation to get caught up in a flurry of activity and spiritual disciplines to live out the Christian life as well as we can; on the other, an assumption that more knowledge equals more holiness and a closer relationship with him. Both miss a very important detail: his presence.

Numerous people have accepted Christ and sought to follow him without recognizing that he is right there all the time. They jump right over Jesus himself and end up in cultural Christianity or a belief system that is true but not relational. There's certainly nothing wrong with more knowledge, acts of service, or spiritual disciplines, but they become empty if he isn't at the heart of them. The entirety of the Christian life is following the living Jesus who is present with us. That's what he called his friends to do. Everything else needs to come as part of that relationship or not at all.

Don't miss the gift of simple friendship with him—a living, active relationship in which you know he is in the room with you at all times. In fact, he's even closer than that, living inside of you. Talk with him, listen to him, get to know him, and even just sit silently with him sometimes. A relationship with him is not an activity or a system of thought. It's a reality you are invited to experience and enjoy every day of your life.

Q: The idea of a relationship with Jesus is common among his followers, but actually relating to him as a present person is less common. Why do you think recognizing the difference is important? In what ways have you tried to relate to him in the past? What is the difference between being religious and following Jesus? What implications does each have for the way you live? Which do you think is more likely to transform your life into something that resembles him?

"[Many people] miss the secret power that very few possess.
This is the power that the disciples in Acts and the epistles experienced.
Wherever they went, and whenever they touched other lives, they gave
the impression of adequacy for any situation that might arise.
This adequacy wasn't found in a mentality of trying harder but of having
been with Jesus. That is the secret power."
—Leslie Weatherhead

And they will call him Immanuel (which means "God with us").

MATTHEW 1:23

25
JESUS IN THE CHAIR

Try an experiment. During your time of prayer and reflection, as you're starting your day out with Jesus, pull up a chair facing you and envision Jesus sitting there with you. Talk to him as though he is in the chair, just as you would talk to a friend who is physically present. Ask him whatever you want to ask him, and listen to whatever you think he might be saying back to you. Carry on as though he is genuinely in the room.

Now reflect on that experience. Was it just your imagination? Or perhaps this is a better question: *Was it true?* If Jesus is with you always—if he knows your thoughts and hears your voice and walks with you throughout your day—then your exercise was not a matter of trying to convince yourself of something that isn't real. You were convincing yourself of something very true. The reality is that the same Jesus who walked the earth two millennia ago is sitting with you right now.

That's an amazing thought, isn't it? It's also an important one to keep in mind—to "practice" his presence daily—as you walk with him. The relationship that transforms our lives is not very transforming when we aren't even aware of how real and alive that relationship is. Following Jesus is not just a matter of reading and memorizing his Word or praying in times of need, as important as those are. It's a matter of experiencing him in daily life—in all the ups and downs, the busyness and the quiet moments. Make that experience your focus and talk to him as often as you like. And always feel free to pull up a chair.

Q: Start out today with the same exercise that began yesterday. Have you begun to feel that Jesus is in the room or walking with you when you talk to him? What is this experience like? Why do you think pulling up a chair helps create a sense of Jesus' presence? Why is this more than just an act of imagination?

"You can have imagination without faith,
but you can't have faith without imagination."
—Leslie Weatherhead

*We have been released
from the law so that we serve
in the new way of the Spirit,
and not in the old way of the
written code.*

ROMANS 7:6

26
PLAYING THE JESUS WAY

The last few weeks, we have focused on the core of our new life in Jesus—developing a real, interactive relationship with him. No matter how long we have known him and followed him, we need to keep coming back to this foundational truth. This what our life is all about now. We listen to our Caddy and Friend, we grow in our relationship with him, and we experience his presence daily. And that prepares us to play the course less played the way he intended.

One of the first things to realize when we play this magnificent course is that, having accepted Jesus' scorecard as our own, par is no longer a very important standard. God doesn't expect us to reach the ideal score for his course any more than an amateur golfer would be expected to shoot in the high 60s or low 70s like the pros do. He wants us to improve and grow over time, but he doesn't start us out with an impossible standard that would only lead to frustration. He coaches us toward a goal that is right for us at the moment. In other words, he meets us where we are.

Just as the Old Pro taught Paul McAllister to set his own par—reachable goals that would represent improvement for him—Jesus patiently leads us into new areas of growth. If we need a mulligan on every shot, he gives it. Letting go of our obsession with results—what we will call a NATO (Not Attached to Outcome) approach—we swing and live more freely, and our game and lives improve. We draw closer to the Caddy and fulfill the designer's purpose for our lives when we learn to play the Jesus way.

Q: In what areas of your life have you been driven by goals in the past? What benefits does this approach have? What frustrations come with it? How can unrealistic goals hinder your improvement rather than helping it?

"To be forever striving to play perfect golf when you are playing good golf is natural enough but inclined to lead to disaster. Contentment forms a big item in the temperamental makeup of the great player."
—Jack White

The fruit of the Spirit is
love, joy, peace, forbearance,
kindness, goodness, faithfulness,
gentleness and self-control.

GALATIANS 5:22-23

27
CHOOSE THE RIGHT CLUBS

As you might expect, the course less played requires a different approach not only with your scoring but also with your equipment. You have in your bag a remarkable assortment of clubs. Some of them will keep you in bounds and out of trouble. Others will help you get out of the trouble you've managed to find. All of them have the power to advance the designer's purposes in your life and the lives of your playing partners.

The most essential of these clubs are foundational truths, like God's unshakeable, overwhelming love for you, the assurance of his complete and permanent forgiveness, his ongoing presence with you and in you, and the reliability of his Word and its promises, among others. But you also have nine clubs in your bag that reflect God's own nature: love, joy, peace, patience, kindness, goodness, faithfulness, gentleness, and self-control. These are the fruit of his Spirit within you, and whether you feel like they are part of your nature or not, they are present and will grow as you continue to walk with Jesus. These are the characteristics that make you resemble him.

Remember that your Caddy is not a typical caddy; he will help you with this growth process. Not only will he remind you of the clubs you need to use; he will also empower you to use them. You will need to know them, choose them in each moment, and put them into practice. They should shape every stroke you make. They make beautiful shots once you've learned to use them well, and they are a pleasure for your playing partners to behold. They will enhance your game, enrich your life, and transform the world around you in remarkable ways.

Q: Can you think of situations in life in which you have "used the wrong club"—when you've responded to someone with the wrong attitude, misread someone's intentions, or tried to get someone to do what you wanted in a way that was unproductive? What other "clubs" might you have used in those situations?

"Golf . . . is the infallible test. The man who can go into a patch of rough alone, with the knowledge that only God is watching him, and play his ball where it lies, is the man who will serve you faithfully and well."
—P.G. Wodehouse

Faith is confidence in what we hope for and assurance about what we do not see.

HEBREWS 11:1

28
ENVISION YOUR SHOT

Jack Nicklaus used to "go to the movies" before he hit a shot. He would stand behind the ball, look down the fairway, and imagine being in a theater watching himself make the perfect shot. During his practice swing, he would "see" and "feel" the shot happening, sometimes even saying under his breath, "That was a good one."

The body tends to follow what the mind sees. That's why you can't overcome slices, hooks, or shanks—or sins or failures—by thinking about how much you don't want them to happen. The mind doesn't discern "don't" in your mental images. It just sees the picture, positive or negative, and directs your body toward it. With a mind that believes what you tell it so easily, it makes sense to tell it something good. It is absolutely essential to have a positive vision if you want your shot—or your life—to follow it.

If your mind is that responsive to the images you put in it, you have a lot of say over how your life goes. When your fears fill your thoughts with negative possibilities, you can replace them with something much more in line with God's will for you. When you're consumed with regret about the past, you can turn your attention to the future, knowing that God has good plans for it. This isn't magic; you still face challenges in life. But it can keep you from sabotaging your own faith with thoughts that contradict it.

Live your life like Nicklaus played golf. Focus your mind on where you need to go, envision the steps that get you there, think through the execution, then visualize it and "experience" it in your mind. That's faith, and it's powerful. It's the only way to reach God's purposes for your life.

Q: What kinds of things do you tell your mind when you play golf? How do you think your game would change if your pre-shot routine was to feed it nothing but positive images of beautiful shots (even when you're presented with contrary evidence)? How might this principle of a pre-shot routine apply to other areas of your life?

"Concepts and visualizations stored in your mind's eye
are the most important keys in golf."
—Mike Hebron

Whatever is true,
whatever is noble,
whatever is right,
whatever is pure,
whatever is lovely,
whatever is admirable—
if anything is excellent
or praiseworthy—
think about such things.

PHILIPPIANS 4:8

29
NATO GOLF

If your goal in golf is a good score, you will play with a constant focus on results—having a good round overall, getting birdies and pars on each hole, making the perfect shot with each swing. It's a natural instinct. To get a good result, it seems obvious to think about results. But our obsession with the outcome often has a negative effect. It produces a mentality and a tension that are harmful to our game.

Some of the best amateur golfers are those who have adopted a NATO approach—Not Attached To Outcome. They play without concern for their score, focusing instead on swinging freely and enjoying the game. They work on their mechanics on the range, but they play without pressure. And their scores improve much more rapidly than if they were focused on them.

When you play golf and live life with that kind of freedom, you can let go of a fixation on negative possibilities—what you don't want to happen—and replace them with positive expectations. Surprisingly, the outcomes flow much more naturally and are much more satisfying. You begin to live with freedom and hope, attitudes that, when paired together, can revolutionize the way you live.

What would that look like in your work decisions? In your relationships? In your personal life? Spend some time imagining the possibilities. Don't fixate on certain possibilities as necessary outcomes; just embrace the freedom to be yourself in every area of your life and enjoy the process. Your relationships, work, and personal life will benefit greatly, at least eventually if not right away. And you'll find yourself moving in attitudes and directions you never thought possible. It will transform who you are and how you live.

Q: If you're like many people, you may be highly attached to outcomes and impatient with yourself in growth processes. But try today to set yourself free from those expectations. What would it look like to "swing freely"— not recklessly or carelessly, but in your newfound hope and restfulness—in your work decisions? In your relationships? In your personal life?

"Keep your sense of humor.
There's enough stress in the rest of your life not to let bad shots
ruin a game you're supposed to enjoy."
—Amy Alcott

If we confess our sins,
he is faithful and just and
will forgive us our sins
and purify us from all
unrighteousness.

1 JOHN 1:9

30
A RELATIONAL PROBLEM

If you've received the Ultimate Mulligan—that perfect scorecard of Jesus in place of your own—all your mistakes and failures are covered. Those things were relevant to your old scorecard, but you tore that one up when you accepted Jesus' scorecard in its place. The biblical word for all our shots in life that missed the mark is sin. The word carries all kinds of religious connotations and makes people think of rules they can't live up to. And though that's true—sin means not living up to God's rules—this is no longer our burden. Jesus did live up to those rules, and his scorecard proves it.

But it's still important for us to understand what sin is because we still do it sometimes. We make bad shots in golf and in life. Contrary to popular belief, sin is not primarily a performance problem. It is reflected in our actions, but the source is not simply behavioral. It is a relational issue. It indicates a decision—even a subconscious or habitual one—to play our own course instead of God's. It's a symptom of living independently, whether out of pride, fear, or insecurity. It shows us that we have gone our own way and are experiencing the consequences, and it serves as a warning to get back to the course God designed.

The good news is that God does not hold our sins against us if we have already accepted Jesus' scorecard. But he does want us to recognize them, confess them, and have our relationship with him restored. His grace is infinitely greater than any and all sins we have ever committed, and all we have to do is ask for it. He immediately restores us to walk the course made just for the Son and his friends.

Q: Why does playing with no pressure—the awareness that God gives ample mulligans—have the effect of improving our game rather than making it worse? Why do we need fewer and fewer mulligans as we continue to play with Jesus as our Caddy?

"We will continue to sin, but the key to life is to realize that God
accepts our misses and forgives them. Yet his desire for us is that
we make progress and miss less—that there is improvement in all areas
of our game, from our short game to our long game. The key is to realize
that we aren't expected to be perfect but to be making progress.
Our progress then needs to be measured by the risk that we are taking
as we step onto the thin ice of life and trust him."
—Wally Armstrong

Forgetting what is behind and
straining toward what is ahead,
I press on toward the goal
to win the prize for which
God has called me heavenward
in Christ Jesus.

PHILIPPIANS 3:13-14

31
THE HAZARD OF REGRET

In his golf game, Paul McAllister proved he could hit all his shots when he had a mulligan to back him up. Sometimes the best shot didn't come on the first try, but with the pressure off and second chances on every stroke, it became clear that the problem wasn't his ability. He simply needed some mulligans.

What if you could do life like that? What if every time you made a mistake—a bad business decision, a rude comment, a kneejerk reaction—you took a mulligan instead of beating yourself up? Like Paul, you might start to live with more confidence and make more solid shots than ever. You'd learn from your mistakes rather than letting them plague your thoughts. You would enjoy life, feel more freedom, and make better decisions.

That's the opportunity God gives us again and again. The Creator of second chances does not want us to keep looking back at the chances we missed. He gave us the perfect scorecard so we would no longer live with regret, wishing we could rewrite our past. He wants us to be free from the weight of yesterday's mistakes and live with joy. And the only way to do that is to receive forgiveness no matter how often we need it.

That isn't easy for many of us, but it's an essential part of following Jesus. Your past can help explain the present—the attitudes and actions that affect your life now—but it doesn't have to determine your future. The whole point of forgiveness is to liberate us from sins and failures we could never overcome on our own. Receive that gift whenever and wherever it is needed.

Q: To what degree has regret been a problem for you? Do you tend to look back and wish life had been different? What do God's mulligans mean for your past and your future?

"When you think about it, a whole round is made up of mulligans.
Therefore, the one who learns to let go of the past and step forward
to the shot at hand will win many a match."
—Wally Armstrong

Let us draw near to God
with a sincere heart and
with the full assurance
that faith brings,
having our hearts sprinkled to
cleanse us from
a guilty conscience and
having our bodies washed
with pure water.

HEBREWS 10:22

32
THE HAZARD OF SELF-PROTECTION

Having an awful round of golf can be embarrassing. An ill-timed chunk, a putt that comes up ridiculously short, a snap hook into the woods next to a wide-open fairway—these are moments that make you want to run and hide. Especially if you're playing with golfers who are better than you—or even your Caddy, who has a perfect scorecard who might have expected to see more improvement in your game.

As we've seen, Jesus doesn't expect us to have a perfect scorecard, and he's patient with our growth process. That's why he gave us his scorecard in the first place. But sometimes we still want to run and hide when we sin because we're ashamed of what we did. We knew we would fall short of his standard, but perhaps we didn't expect to fall *this* short. Like a child caught in a disobedient act, we avoid eye contact, cover our tracks, or even deny we did anything wrong. We land in the hazard of self-protection. Sometimes we just want to run away.

Avoiding intimacy with God may be a natural instinct, but it's the wrong one. When you sin, let your first response be to run toward him—to remember that he offers unlimited mulligans, to rekindle the conversations you've had with him, to put the past behind and press ahead with joy. Vulnerability is an essential aspect of a true friendship, and it applies both in your relationship with Jesus and in your relationships with other people. You don't need to protect yourself with him, and if you've avoided the trap of other people's opinions, you don't need to protect yourself from them either. Have a talk with Jesus and receive his forgiveness. Play another mulligan and enjoy your round.

Q: When we blow it with God, we want to run and hide, just as the first human beings did when they disobeyed him (Genesis 3:8). What circumstances have caused you to feel that way about God? Why is that instinct harmful to your fellowship with him? Under what circumstances have you experienced a self-protective instinct with other people? How has that affected your relationships?

"Reverse every natural instinct and do the opposite of what
you are inclined to do, and you will probably come very close to
having a perfect golf swing."
—Ben Hogan

*Do not be anxious about
anything, but in every situation,
by prayer and petition,
with thanksgiving,
present your requests to God.
And the peace of God, which
transcends all understanding,
will guard your hearts and your
minds in Christ Jesus.*

PHILIPPIANS 4:6

33
THE HAZARD OF WORRIES AND FEARS

Nothing ruins your enjoyment of the game—or your ability to swing freely—more than anxiety. It freezes your body, clouds your decisions, and drains you of energy. It causes you to see every fairway as narrow and every hazard and rough as huge. It practically convinces you that you're going to hit a bad shot, even if you've hit the same shot successfully many times before.

Our worries and fears on the golf course can come from many sources: the opinion of our playing partners, the pressure we put on ourselves to record a low score, or the seeming impatience of that faster group pushing us from behind. But in life, the sources are endless. We worry about all kinds of hazards in our future and wonder how things will turn out. Our anxiety brings the emotional impact of those potential problems into our present, even though they remain the future and many will never occur. Our faith weakens as our fears rise, and we're caught in a trap we don't know how to escape from.

How do we avoid the hazard of anxiety? One way is to focus on the target, not the adversity or the potential problems. Fears magnify the negative, turning life's ponds into oceans and its bunkers into vast deserts. Filling our vision with the opportunity rather than the obstacle has the opposite effect. But it's even better to focus on the problem-solver, the course designer who knew about all your obstacles before he even created the course. There is nothing too big for God, no situation Jesus cannot overcome. Listen to the words of your Caddy as he stirs up your faith. He knows the way out, over, around, or through, and he is faithful to lead you there.

Q: How prone to worry and fear are you? What kinds of things do you tend to worry about? What would you identify as your biggest concern for the future right now? To what degree do you think your worries and fears have affected your decisions? Your relationships? Your sense of contentment? Your health?

THE HAZARD OF WORRIES AND FEARS

"For this game you need, above all things,
to be in a tranquil frame of mind."
—Harry Vardon

*"I will repay you for the years the
locusts have eaten. . . .
You will have plenty to eat,
until you are full, and you will
praise the name of the Lord your
God, who has worked wonders
for you; never again will my
people be shamed."*

JOEL 2:25-26

34
THE HAZARD OF GUILT AND SHAME

It should be clear by now that God deals with our imperfect scorecard by tearing it up and replacing it with Jesus' perfect one, and that we have unlimited mulligans to use as we learn and grow in relationship with him. Our guilt and shame have been undone, and in theory, that should be the end of those heavy burdens. In experience, however, we may still wrestle with the pain of missed opportunities and tragic mistakes. Like Paul McAllister, whose damaged relationships cost him years with his wife and son, we wish our mulligans could take us back in time to avoid our failures in the first place. As with the hazard of regret, the hazard of guilt and shame can keep us trapped in the past.

Shame is an attack on our identity. It tells us not that we've done something bad but that we *are* bad. It causes us to forget that we are made in God's image and completely and overwhelmingly loved by him, and it ignores the full forgiveness we have been given. It doesn't belong on life's course less played, but we find ourselves caught in it anyway. It's a devastating blow to our self-image as new creations.

The best way to play out of the hazard of guilt and shame is to trust that God can redeem any situation and restore any loss we've experienced. He can rebuild relationships, cause missed opportunities to come around again, and make the restoration of our lives even better than the original plan. Our trust must be anchored in his forgiveness, but it must also look forward to his creative solutions. He has removed our guilt and shame as far as the east is from the west, and he never wants us to feel those pains again.

Q: What mistakes, habits, or failures in your past or present cause you to feel shame? What have they cost you relationally and emotionally? If you heard Jesus promise you today, "I will more than make up for all the losses you have ever experienced," how would you respond? What losses would come to mind first?

The Hazard of Guilt and Shame

"Golf is about how well you accept, respond to, and score with your misses
much more so than it is a game of your perfect shots."
—Dr. Bob Rotella

Therefore encourage one another
and build each other up,
just as in fact you are doing.

1 THESSALONIANS 5:11

35
PLAY TOGETHER

The relationships that develop on the golf course are among the greatest benefits of the game. People who love the sport and enjoy playing together often form lasting bonds of friendship. It's a unique opportunity to interact, encourage, celebrate, speak the same language, laugh at the same frustrations, and carry on a friendly competition. Building relationships through the game make it fun and rewarding.

But a lot can happen to undermine relationships on the course—like too much focus on the scores, too much aggravation over missed shots, or too much competitiveness and pride. When we make the game about results, we miss the best part.

As we've seen, that happens in life all the time. If we aren't careful, we become preoccupied with productivity and outcomes and tasks, neglecting our relationships with the people we love. We get too busy to share our heart or let others share theirs with us. We become competitive with coworkers or neighbors and lose our compassion for other human beings going through the same struggles we face. We turn conversations into transactions and never see the needs around us. We stop investing our lives in others and expecting them to invest in us. We simply forget to enjoy the people we play with.

If life is all about relationships and we make it all about something else, we risk getting to the end and looking back with enormous pain and regret. Make a commitment now to avoid that tragedy. Take time every day, including today, to appreciate the people around you and enjoy their company. Offer some encouragement—a pat on the back, a "nice shot" for a job well done, a smile that shows you're paying attention. The world around you needs that kind of friendship. And, if you're honest, so do you.

Q: What are some of your good intentions that you've never acted on in your relationships? In what ways can you improve on your follow-through? Even in the busyness of your daily schedule, what can you do to enjoy the people around you more? How do you think demonstrating your appreciation in words and actions would affect their lives?

"You are not here in the world for yourself. You have been sent here for others. The world is waiting for you!"
—Catherine Booth

"A new command I give you:
Love one another.
As I have loved you,
so you must love one another."

JOHN 13:34

36
REACH OUT

The Old Pro could have dismissed Paul as a lost cause. Or he could have decided he had better things to do with his time. He could have criticized Paul for his attitude, pushed Paul to make some changes, or gotten impatient and said something rude. But as an experienced follower of Jesus who knew how patient God had been with him, the Old Pro was able to look at other people from God's perspective and recognize their significance and value. He understood what was really important in life and invested himself in relationships.

That's how we come to see life when we spend a lot of time in conversation with our Caddy and Friend. He rubs off on us, and the transformation gives us a new perspective that is no longer all about ourselves. Like the Old Pro, we seek to reflect Jesus by serving others and being available to them. As Jesus has been a friend to us, we learn to build friendships with the people he loves.

Above all others, that includes those closest to us. Our family members need our time and attention because God has put them in our lives to love them and experience their love in return. But it also includes friends, colleagues, acquaintances, and even strangers. Kind words and a gentle spirit go a long way in changing lives. Sometimes the only way the people around us can see Jesus is by looking at his Spirit in us. We need to make sure his love is there to be seen.

God reaches the world through those who follow him. Like the Old Pro, let him reach people through you. Never forget what is truly important. Invest yourself in the people he has put in your life.

Q: What characteristics of friendship did the Old Pro exhibit? Why are these characteristics appealing to us? While it's great to spend time with people we naturally get along with, why might it be important to develop some friendships beyond those boundaries too? What do we have to gain and to give in those relationships?

"If we truly love people, we will desire for them far more than that which is
within our power to give them, and this will lead us to prayer.
Intercession is a way of loving others."
—Richard Foster

Be devoted to one another
in love.
Honor one another
above yourselves.

ROMANS 12:10

37
LOVE IN PRACTICE

"I recently read that the next great evangelistic movement will be a demonstration," Paul told his son. "If you want somebody to be interested in the Lord, you ought to behave differently." In fact, the only way some people are going to see Jesus is if he is evident in our lives. We are the ones who demonstrate what he is like.

By now, you know what kind of friend Jesus is. He freely gives away mulligans, listens to anything you want to tell him, offers his wisdom if you're willing to listen to him, patiently teaches you and gets you out of the hazards of life, and keeps inviting you into the wonderful adventure of the course less played. He doesn't push, pressure, or prod, and he doesn't give up on you when you seem slow to come around. He is a model of patient, enduring love.

That's one thing Paul loved about the Old Pro. Will didn't push him. He challenged him at times, but he didn't resort to pressure. He simply walked beside him as a friend day after day, week after week until Paul was ready to make the decisions that would change his life. And if Paul hadn't made those decisions, we get the sense that the Old Pro would have kept on being his friend anyway. A true friend genuinely cares and hangs in there with you no matter what.

Friendship is what love looks like when put into practice, and we have multiple opportunities to demonstrate it every day. We may not have the time on our hands that the Old Pro had, but we have enough to encourage, challenge, teach, learn, listen, and love. Jesus has been working *in* us; it is time for him to work *through* us too.

Q: What did Paul mean when he told his son the next great evangelistic movement would be a demonstration? What is the connection between the attitudes and actions of those who follow Jesus and the interest other people show toward him?

"It doesn't take a huge spotlight to draw attention to how great our God is.
All it takes is for one committed person to so let his light shine before men
that a world lost in darkness welcomes the light."
—Gary Smalley and John Trent

Be kind and compassionate to
one another,
forgiving each other,
just as in Christ God
forgave you.

EPHESIANS 4:32

38
PASS THE
MULLIGANS ON

If you've been hurt, you know how difficult forgiveness can be. And the deeper the hurts go, the harder it is. Paul McAllister had trouble forgiving his hypercritical, abusive father and the high school coach who abandoned him. Some people never get over the pain of betrayal by a spouse or close friend. We resent harsh words and unexpected slights at home, at work, and wherever else we experience them. The wounds we experience over time build up in our hearts and come out in our words and actions.

Sometimes those wounds turn against us. There can be a strong connection between the pain we've suffered from other people's decisions and the pain we inflict on ourselves for the mistakes we've made. If we feel like we can't forgive them, we will also have trouble forgiving ourselves. You may have seen this dynamic at work; just as Paul called himself an idiot and an embarrassment on the ninth hole, you may be just as unforgiving whenever you make a bad shot in golf or life. You're holding on to judgments against yourself and those who have hurt you.

Whatever it takes, let them go. When God gave you Jesus' scorecard and released you from all your failures and shortcomings, he wiped out the penalty for even the worst mistakes. Now he calls you to do the same for others—to release them from the wrongs they committed. The pain may still be there for now, but if you let him, he will begin to heal it. When you embrace his forgiveness for yourself, really letting it sink in, it becomes much easier to offer forgiveness to those around you. They will see something of God's nature in you, and they too can begin to heal.

Q: Usually when we have trouble forgiving someone (like Paul with his father and his coach), it's because we haven't learned to receive forgiveness for ourselves. When we really embrace God's forgiveness for ourselves and let it sink in, it becomes much easier to offer forgiveness. Have you experienced that dynamic in your life? In what relationships has God begun to heal some of those hurts? In what relationships can you help bring healing by offering your forgiveness?

"I am blessed. I can bless. So this is happiness. . . .
I am a flame to light other flames."
—Ann Voskamp

Let us consider how we may spur one another on toward love and good deeds, not giving up meeting together, as some are in the habit of doing, but encouraging one another.

HEBREWS 10:24-25

39

CATCH SOMEONE DOING SOMETHING RIGHT

As a golfer, you're familiar with the kind encouragement playing partners often give each other during a round. "Great shot." "Beautiful putt." "Nice read." "Ooh, bad break, but I think you're still in pretty good shape." It's a friendly atmosphere, especially when the stakes are low. Friends can relax and spur each other on with ease.

For some reason, that doesn't always carry over into other areas of life. Perhaps the stakes seem higher. A work project, a spouse's approval, a child's grades, a bad habit, a looming deadline, or a financial decision can seem like make-or-break situations that threaten our wellbeing. Still, we can create an encouraging environment even under those circumstances, taking the pressure off and giving others the freedom to grow and enjoy life. We have an ongoing opportunity to help set the tone in every situation we experience.

This doesn't just happen. We have to be intentional about it, just as the Old Pro intentionally and lovingly pursued Paul, asking him compelling questions and then listening to him, smiling, and offering encouragement. He showed interest in Paul's story and offered comfort and compassion when he was hurting. He took the time to build trust between them and trusted God for the results.

Make it a point to work encouragement into your conversations. Catch people doing something right and applaud them for it. At work, affirmation is much better for productivity than pressure and demands. At home, it's essential for the health of your most important relationships. If you make time for conversations and fill them with positive words, you may be amazed at where those conversations go and how they change lives. You may also be amazed at how much more gratifying your own life becomes.

Q: Spend some time envisioning what a culture of affirmation looks like. How do you think creating an environment like that would transform your home? Your workplace? Any other areas of influence in your life?

Catch Someone Doing Something Right

"Dear Lord, stay with us and then we shall begin to shine as you shine. . . .
It will be you shining on others through us."
—Mother Teresa

Love is patient,
love is kind.
It does not envy,
it does not boast,
it is not proud.

1 CORINTHIANS 13:4

40
THE HAZARD OF COMPARISON

In the opening scenes of *The Mulligan*, when Paul was having his worst moments and demonstrating his deepest flaws, you may have noticed a two-sided tendency in his opinions of others. He saw less-experienced golfers as hacks and professionals as models to strive for. He oozed pride toward one group and envy toward the other. Both of these unhealthy attitudes are the product of comparing ourselves with others.

Comparison is a dangerous hazard that is hard to avoid. Most human beings land in it from time to time, and the results are never good. If we compare ourselves favorably with others, we risk becoming arrogant. If we compare ourselves unfavorably, we become envious. Each attitude gives us a distorted self-perception and distracts us from God's view of us. The truth is that we came from the humblest of circumstances and, through God's forgiveness, are given the high privilege of being his children. That perspective rules out both pride and a poor self-image.

To avoid this difficult hazard, you'll need to notice whenever your thoughts start to veer toward it. Whenever you find yourself hoping you're good enough for the people around you or thinking you're better than them, you are comparing. Replace those thoughts with God's view of you—someone made in his image (like everyone else), who is overwhelmingly loved (like everyone else), and who (like everyone else) has a unique personality and purpose in his world that is not exactly like anyone else's. That view acknowledges your incredible value as well as the equal value of those around you. It reminds you that your scorecard was bad and the one you've been given is perfect. And it frees you to simply be you, not measured by any other human being and treasured for who you are.

Q: In what ways does comparison distort our perception of ourselves? How do you think you might have done this at times? How does knowing God's view of us eliminate our need to compare ourselves with others? How does his value for us both honor our uniqueness and significance and remind us of the uniqueness and significance of others?

"One of the most fascinating things about golf is how it reflects the cycle
of life. No matter what you shoot—the next day you have to go back to the
first tee and begin all over again and make yourself into something."
—Peter Jacobsen

May the God of hope fill you with all joy and peace as you trust in him, so that you may overflow with hope by the power of the Holy Spirit.

ROMANS 15:13

41
THE HAZARD OF HOPELESSNESS

You've probably noticed an interesting phenomenon: An encouraging session of tweaking your swing at the driving range fills you with hope for your next round, but old habits return on the course, and those great shots at the range become a distant memory. The reasons for that dynamic are many—different conditions, different lies, and different thought processes and expectations—but the result is the same. You end up disappointed. And if you are disappointed often enough, you begin to lose hope.

That's a small picture of a bigger dynamic in life. We've all experienced disappointments large and small on many occasions, and if we don't know how to get over them, they build up and color our vision of everything. We lose hope, lower expectations, and assume that the doors to our dreams will probably remain closed. Bitterness grows, and life stops being an adventure. It becomes something we just have to endure.

Not everyone gets to that point, of course, but even mild disappointments can give us a skewed perspective on life. It's a subtle hazard, much like a soggy depression in life's fairway. You may not see it until you have to hit out of it. But you do have wonderful clubs in your bag for dealing with it—faith, trust, and hope—and you can use them by relying on God's promises and remembering that with him, your past is not a prediction of your future. He is a master of rewriting stories, of turning the plot in a positive direction in response to your faith in him. Let hope fill your heart and mind as you trust in him, and expect the future to be different from the past. He is leading you to holes you've never played and more beautiful shots than you've ever made.

Q: How does disappointment tend to distort our perspective on all of life? How does it shape our relationship with God? What do you think God would say to you about your biggest disappointments?

The Hazard of Hopelessness

"Resolve never to quit, never to give up, no matter what the situation."
—Jack Nicklaus

"Freely you have received;
freely give."

MATTHEW 10:8

42
BECOMING AN OLD PRO

You've learned a lot from your Caddy and Friend. You've received his wisdom in his Word and in conversations with him, and you've seen it in people like the Old Pro. You have some experience playing on the course less played and have begun to see how rewarding and fulfilling it can be. Like everyone who follows him, you are in the midst of a radical transformation process that has implications for all your relationships and every area of your life.

What do you do with that gift? You have a lifetime and an eternity to enjoy it, and you should. But there's something else you should do with it too. The gift was not only for you; it was also for those who know you. They benefit from what God is doing in your life, and now you have an opportunity to pass it on even further. You can become an Old Pro yourself.

Like the Old Pro, you have a lot to offer those around you. You will encounter people like Paul, whose misplaced priorities were creating lasting, complex issues in his life and relationships. You will also meet people who are hurting, confused, or just wandering. Some people will need a little friendly encouragement or a listening ear, and others will need some in-depth coaching over a longer time. Some are already close to you—your family members and friends who need your support and advice; some are colleagues or acquaintances dealing with stresses or disappointments who need a new perspective; and some are strangers you will meet when the time is right. In every case and in varying degrees, you have something to give. You know the Caddy. Many other people in your world need to know him too.

Q: Think of any mentoring or coaching relationships that have had an impact on your life. How did they change you? What about them was so impactful? What can you do to "pay it forward" and provide that influence for someone else?

"The greatest good you can do for another is not just to share your riches
but to reveal to him his own."
—Benjamin Disraeli

As iron sharpens iron,
so one person sharpens another.

PROVERBS 27:17

43
ONE OF LIFE'S MOST CHALLENGING SHOTS

Mentors like the Old Pro know how to encourage, but they also know how to speak uncomfortable truths. While people need an environment of encouragement and affirmation in order to grow, they are sometimes involved in behavioral habits, thought patterns, and relational dynamics that have harmful effects and keep them from growing. They may know something is wrong, but they aren't sure how to fix it, or even exactly what the problem is in the first place. They need someone to point it out, even if they may resent the words that do so.

Correction from a trusted friend can have a lifechanging effect. If the friend is personally affected by that person's attitudes or actions, correction may come in the form of a rebuke of the wrong and forgiveness for the damage it has done. In either case, it's an interaction filled with potential dangers—a bad reaction or short-term resentment, perhaps, or even a broken friendship in worst-case scenarios. But a true friend takes that risk for the good of the other, knowing that speaking the truth in love can have a lifechanging effect and break down the strongest barriers people have placed around their hearts.

Any relationship, by the very nature of our interactions, can sharpen us by revealing our attitudes and perspectives and the need for change. Some people have a sandpaper effect of softening our hard edges by stretching our patience and love. But trusted friends or partners can go further than most in speaking truth into each other's lives, and we are wise to make room for that in those relationships. We grow—and help others grow—by considering observations and insights spoken with a little courage and a lot of honesty.

Q: Who in your past has spoken difficult truths to you? How did it go over? Looking back with perspective, why was it important for you to hear that from someone you trusted? In what ways can you build trust in your relationships that creates the right context for honest, challenging words when needed? How do relationships reach that level of honesty?

"One reason golf is such an exasperating game is that a thing we learned
is so easily forgotten, and we find ourselves struggling year after year with
faults we had discovered and corrected time and again."
—Bobby Jones

You were taught . . .
to be made new in the attitude
of your minds; and to put on the
new self, created to be like God
in true righteousness
and holiness.

EPHESIANS 4:22-24

44
THE BIG PICTURE

We've walked through many components of the life of faith so far this year, but it's important to realize that this life is not just made up of its parts. It's an integrated whole, and it's best to see it as a mental image instead of thinking about it as a lot of instructions. In fact, each aspect of a swing movement can correspond to an aspect of our life of faith (see illustrations).

Many golfers make the mistake of thinking that their swing is a series of connected parts, but it's really a flow of connected movements. It should be a timed sequence, a symphony rather than a melody, a chain of events rather than a bunch of links.

That's a great picture of the life of faith. Most believers are performance-driven, focusing on improving the different parts of their life, rather than being driven by love as the moving force behind it all. We grow not by compartmentalizing life and working on the compartments but by living with the same mental image of love for everything. Our friendship with Jesus sets us up for that perfectly. Just as a unified, rotational circle is the image we hold in our minds when we swing the club, Jesus is the image we hold in our minds as we go through our daily lives.

When we are driven by a holistic mental image, whether for our golf swing or our life, the result is balance. We become well-rounded, playing golf and life the way the course is supposed to be played. The simplicity of a single image keeps our focus on our purpose rather than our performance, and we are free to enjoy the game. Our play and our lives flow just as they should.

Q: When we are trying to improve our golf swing, we tend to make the most progress by "seeing" it in our minds rather than trying to improve a part of the movement within it. Why do you think it's important to see your life this way too? In what ways has envisioning Jesus and spending time with him helped you to do this?

"Nothing verbal can replace an intelligent visual conception of the swing."
—Percy Boomer

These two sketches use a wagon wheel to illustrate a principle. In order to effectively pull a cart, all the spokes must be balanced and supported by the hub, which supplies the inner power. If any spoke is damaged, it will destroy the functionality of the wheel.

This sketch is the balanced follower's walk with God, encircled by his Love and Forgiveness with all of the spokes (Prayer, God's Word, Fellowship, Friendship, Jesus) synchronized in a solid, functioning relationship with God. Any one of these spokes that is either weak or not practiced will destroy an effective walk. The foundational picture for a follower of Jesus must always be to envision their life encircled by God's love and forgiveness.

This sketch is the balanced circular golf swing, with all of the spokes (Grip, Stance, Backswing, Forward Swing, Spine Angle) synchronized in a solid, functioning golf swing. Any one of these spokes that is either weak or not practiced will destroy an effective swing. The foundational picture for the golfer must always be to envision the golf club swinging in a circle around the spine.

*I pray that you, being rooted and
established in love,
may have power, together with
all the Lord's holy people,
to grasp how wide and long
and high and deep
is the love of Christ,
and to know this love that
surpasses knowledge—that you
may be filled to the measure of
all the fullness of God.*

EPHESIANS 3:17-19

45
THE RIM OF LOVE

The golf swing should make a circle. It may go against our instincts to swing in a circle to make something go straight, and we tend to modify that arc to make the ball do what we want it to do. But natural instincts and common sense aren't always reliable in golf or in life. Sometimes we have to set aside our human reasoning to follow the truth we've been given. That requires faith.

In life, we receive God's love and continue to live in it by faith. We must realize we were created to be swung by God and are firmly in his grip. We become aware that we have a living, interactive relationship with him through his Son, Jesus. We are constantly encircled by his love and forgiveness, and we respond by the power of his Spirit to love ourselves as he loves us and love others as we have been loved. We are always surrounded by the arc of his loving, forgiving presence.

That's where our mental image begins, and it fits with the way we are designed. The golf club is designed to swing in a circle, and we can't swing it well unless we align ourselves with its face and trust the design. The same is true in our spiritual life. We are designed to be held by God and moved by his love. He will never let us go, but his swing won't have its full effect unless we trust him. We can't accomplish anything by understanding the mechanics. We must simply see the picture of his love in Jesus and move as he leads us. When we do, we live as loved followers of Jesus in action, ready to be used by him.

Q: The golf swing doesn't have to be complex to be effective. Neither does the life of faith. How does knowing God's love simplify everything else in our walk with him? In what ways does it go against human reasoning to believe in God's love for us and receive his unlimited forgiveness? Why is faith important to maintain our fellowship with him?

THE RIM OF LOVE

"The only thing that really matters is the design of the club.
In fact, the design of the golf club is the only master model of the golf
swing. When you let the design of the club design your swing concept,
your body will fall into symptomatic compliance."
—Charles Hogan

*"If you remain in me and
my words remain in you,
ask whatever you wish,
and it will be done for you."*

JOHN 15:17

46
THE GRIP OF
PRAYER

The placement of the hands on the club's grip is the only connection between the player and the game. If that isn't right, the rest of the swing is in trouble. The position of the hands and the tension of the hand's muscles affect the trajectory of the swing and therefore the trajectory of the ball. The grip is the heartbeat of every shot.

Prayer is the heartbeat of the believer's life. It is the ongoing connection between us and God, and it affects everything we do. Like a grip on the club, our conversations with God form a link between his will for us and the trajectory of our lives. When our prayers are too loose, too tight, or out of alignment—in other words, if we are not praying much, praying in an effort to control everything, or praying outside of his will—the movements of our life are affected. Our prayers are vital points of contact between God's wisdom, power, and love and the situations and circumstances of our lives.

We have been given many rock-solid promises for our prayers. God promises to hear us and to answer. If we align ourselves with his Word and his will and ask him in faith, we can be sure he will respond at the right time and in the right ways. He even promises to shape our desires and prayers if we let him. Prayer is not a matter of trying to get what we want but wanting what we get. As we have seen, our conversations with him are not limited to certain topics; we can talk with him about anything. As we share our concerns and listen for his voice, we grow in confidence that he holds us and our world in his hands.

Q: Nothing can change the fact that you are connected to God as a follower of Jesus, but your experience of that connection can change from day to day. How do your conversations with God maintain that awareness of your connection? How do they connect his wisdom, power, and love with the relationships and circumstances of our lives?

"You can talk to God because God listens. Your voice matters in heaven. He takes you very seriously. When you enter his presence, the attendants turn to you to hear your voice. No need to fear that you will be ignored. Even if you stammer or stumble, even if what you have to say impresses no one, it impresses God—and he listens."

—Max Lucado

*The word of God is alive
and active. Sharper than any
double-edged sword,
it penetrates even to dividing
soul and spirit, joints and
marrow; it judges the thoughts
and attitudes of the heart.*

HEBREWS 4:12

47
A STANCE ON THE WORD

Your stance as you address the ball affects nearly every aspect of your stroke. If you are not correctly aligned, your direction will be off. If you don't distribute your weight properly, you risk mishitting the ball. If your posture isn't based on rotating around your spine, you will not swing in a smooth circle. If your knees and waist are not athletically bent, you lose leverage against the ground. And if your head is not aligned and steady, the moving parts of your swing get out of sync. In other words, your stance affects your balance, stability, power, and direction—all the critical components of a golf shot.

That's how the Word of God applies to our lives. It gives us balance, stability, power, and direction. There is nothing like God's Word for showing us the way to salvation through faith in Jesus and the way to live in his wisdom, power, and love in our daily lives. His Word is alive, inspired by his Spirit, reaching into the depths of our soul to discern our motives, root out our false perspectives, correct our mistakes, and train us in the right way to live. It gives us all the course information for the course less played, as well as the rules for the game. Like a solid stance, it directs every aspect of our game.

That's why it is so important to immerse ourselves in the truth of God's Word as part of our preparation for each day. It sets the tone for and becomes the basis of our conversation with our Caddy—how we hear from him and what we talk to him about. It fills our hearts and minds with his purposes and keeps us on the right course.

Q: In what ways does God's Word, the Bible, give us balance, stability, power, and direction? What does this tell us about the importance of making it a part of our lives each day?

"The most dramatic and permanent declines in handicap occur
when a golfer learns the incorrect concept of the swing.
Golfers don't fail because they're clumsy. They fail because they
misunderstand the use of the golf club."
—Manuel de la Torre

*"Where two or three gather
in my name,
there am I with them."*

MATTHEW 18:20

48
THE BACKSWING OF FELLOWSHIP

Imagine playing golf with a group of friends who come from different backgrounds but all get along and love the game like you do. Your goal when you play is not to see who ends up with the best score. This is not a competition. The goal is to see every player reach a personal best—to have the lowest composite score possible. Now add to that picture a fifth player: the creator of the course who is always on it and loves hanging out with groups like yours. You realize that Jesus *your* Caddy is also Jesus *our* Caddy. What has often been an individual experience for you is now a collective experience filled with warmth, joy, laughter, support, encouragement, and, when needed, challenging words to spur each other on to a better game.

This fellowship of mutual support and accountability is like your backswing. It's where you store up energy, gather momentum, and prepare to launch your swing. Even though it isn't the swing itself, it sets you up for success, so it's important to pay attention to it. You'll want to make sure it isn't rushed and that it takes you all the way to the top of your motion. It will stretch you—the further the better—so don't resist the pull. Your partners in support and accountability are indispensable.

Be sure to bring the main partner into that fellowship. He is already there, of course, but it is important to always be aware of his presence and honor it in your words and interactions. After all, he is the reason for fellowship in the first place. He will fill it with his love and, through the energy it brings, empower all the swings of your life.

Q: What do you enjoy most about a round of golf with friends who enjoy each other's company? How does that fellowship build you up and make you feel valued? What can you do to bring the same experience you have with friends on a golf course into other areas of your life? How might that mutual support and accountability apply to your other relationships?

"You can never establish a personal relationship without
opening up your own heart."
—Paul Tournier

In your hearts revere Christ as Lord. Always be prepared to give an answer to everyone who asks you to give the reason for the hope that you have. But do this with gentleness and respect.

1 PETER 3:15

49

THE FORWARD SWING OF FRIENDSHIP

The most important part of your swing is the swing itself. That may seem obvious, but with so much golf instruction emphasizing the minutest details of setup and mechanics—those individual components that many people see as a series of events rather than a fluid movement—the moment of impact often gets lost in the discussion. But this is what determines the results. Everything else leads to that moment.

We have seen again and again that life is all about relationships. Our friendships are the context for what God is doing in our lives. The work he does within us depends on our relationship with him, and we grow through the relationships he has given us with other people. But that internal growth has many outward implications. Whatever he has poured into us should flow out into our friendships. We become his agents for sharing himself with the world.

As Peter wrote in today's verse, that begins with worship—reverence in our hearts for Christ as Lord. Our worshipful relationship with him makes a difference in our lives, and people may ask us why we live with hope, peace, and joy. So we need to be prepared to give an answer, and even develop friendships with people who need that answer, just as the Old Pro did with Paul McAllister. The purpose of our friendships is not just to get a result; Jesus wants to bring about change in our lives, but he doesn't give up the friendship if we are slow in responding. We too develop our friendships simply for the sake of friendship. But because we live with the Caddy daily, he will be there. We bring him into our relationships. And wherever he is, the blessings and benefits of his kingdom come.

Q: What does it mean to be a real friend? How did the Old Pro exemplify this kind of friendship? What qualities do you desire in a friend?

"Our goal is sharing and showing love within the community
where God has placed us and inviting others
into the incredible friendship that Jesus offers."
—Wally Armstrong

I have been crucified with Christ
and I no longer live,
but Christ lives in me.
The life I now live in the body,
I live by faith in the Son of God,
who loved me and
gave himself for me.

GALATIANS 2:20

50
THE HUB OF FAITH

Many followers of Jesus can relate to a lifestyle of trying to please him with hard work and rule-keeping. That's what most religion is about—trying to live up to the standards and grow through self-discipline. But this is a frustrating way to live because it is based on the willpower and efforts of flawed human beings. The whole reason Jesus came was because our scorecard would never be good enough. No amount of effort is going to meet the highest standards. So if that lifestyle of self-effort didn't work before we met our Caddy and Friend, why would it work afterward? It wouldn't. We received Jesus' scorecard by faith, and we continue to live by faith in his promise to live and work within us.

Faith is what puts Jesus at the center of our swing. From beginning to end, we rely on him. We are no longer driven by perfectionism or people's opinions, no longer trying to fill the empty places in our lives with accomplishments and status, and no longer striving to become somebody significant. We trust in the fact that Jesus' scorecard is sufficient, that God's opinion of us is good and all we need, that he fills up our emptiness with his fullness, and we are already as significant as we can get in his eyes. There's nothing left for us to do to prove ourselves. We simply believe and live from that belief.

A swing driven by insecurities and pressures makes for bad golf. Good golf only happens when a swing is confident and free. The same is true of life, and that's what faith accomplishes for us. It is the basis for everything in our new life, brings all its components into one whole, and gives us all the confidence and freedom we need.

THE MULLIGAN JOURNAL

Q: Love surrounds us always, but faith is at the center of our swing. Why do you think this is the hub on which everything in our life with Jesus depends? In what ways does faith make you confident and free to live life—to play the course less played—the way God intended? Whenever you find your faith weakening or loosening, what do you do to rekindle it?

212

"God may be invisible, but he's in touch. You may not be able to see him,
but he is in control. And that includes you—your circumstances.
That includes what you've just lost. That includes what you've just gained.
That includes all of life—past, present, future."
—Charles Swindoll

*Let us run with perseverance
the race marked out for us,
fixing our eyes on Jesus,
the pioneer and perfecter
of faith.*

HEBREWS 12:1-2

51
THE PURPOSE IS THE PROCESS

Life on the course less played over the last year has covered a lot of terrain. It has centered on Jesus our Caddy and explored why we need him, how we invite him into our lives, how we continue to live in relationship with him, the implications of that relationship for all our other relationships, and the hazards we need to avoid along the way. It is a life filled with adventure, and it is only the beginning. The course less played lasts a lifetime.

You have probably noticed some adversity on this course. It's a beautiful and rewarding course, but it isn't easy. Your old attitudes will creep back in at times and turn your attention back to outcomes and approvals, and you will still have some work to do in restoring broken relationships or reprogramming your mind to envision what is true and good in your future. No one masters the Master's course, and it's important for you to remember that you aren't there for that purpose. Your goal is to be free, to grow, to enjoy, and to pass it on. You'll want to keep getting better, but you must resist condemning yourself when you take a step or two back.

Remember that the end with God is the process itself, not the results. You already have Jesus' perfect scorecard in your hand, so there's no point in working on an alternate one. Just do what you can for your life to line up with his and relax. Trust and believe in his purposes for you. Deal with adversity as it comes, but always in faith. Not an inch of the course less played is beyond the Caddy's reach, and none of your swings is beyond repair. Keep your focus on him and play your heart out.

Q: In what ways have you noticed old ways creeping into your life as a new creation? What tools do you have in place for dealing with those setbacks? From what you've learned throughout this journal, why is it more important to keep your focus not on any recurring mistakes but on continuing to play the course less played with love, joy, and freedom?

"The golf swing is not at all difficult, you'll find that once you understand the conception of the swing as a natural motion, you'll make rapid progress. There's no need to suffer on the course. Golf can be a real joy. But you need to understand what you are trying to do. You cannot change effectively unless you have a clear image of what you are trying to do."
—George Knudson

I have fought the good fight,
I have finished the race,
I have kept the faith.
Now there is in store for me the
crown of righteousness, which
the Lord, the righteous Judge,
will award to me on that day—
and not only to me, but also to
all who have longed
for his appearing.

2 TIMOTHY 4:7-8

52
FINISHING WELL

At the end of the course, what will you be known for? If you could write your epitaph, what would you want it to say? The Old Pro longed to hear, "Well done, Will Dunn." The goal of every follower of Jesus is to hear a "well done" too. Even though we already hold Jesus' perfect scorecard in our hand—our acceptance is not at stake—we want to know we've been faithful to him throughout our lives.

What does it take to hear that response from the Lord? Not perfection; we've seen again and again that he is not expecting us to arrive at some mistake-free way of life. Neither is he adding up our good deeds and subtracting our bad ones, nor is he expecting us to impress the world with our spirituality or bear more fruit in our lives than anyone else. In fact, he is not comparing our life to anyone else's. He only wants us to walk out the calling he has given us, to keep our focus on him, and to follow wherever he leads. If we are faithful in that, we will hear a "well done."

Live with that end goal in mind. Let all your todays be shaped by that face-to-face meeting with the Lord one day in the future. Always remember that he is listening attentively to all you say to him, he is full of grace and forgiveness, he is with you every step of the way with his encouragement and love. When you stand before him one day at the end of your life, it won't be your first time. He is standing with you now. Live for his "well done" today and every day. You will certainly hear it when you have finished the course less played.

Q: Are you living now in a way that is consistent with how you want to be remembered? If not, what is standing in your way? What decisions do you need to make today to end up with the fruitfulness you have and the legacy you want to leave?

"I think it's more than whether or not you win or lose.
It's having that opportunity on that final round, final nine,
to come down the stretch with a chance to win."
—Phil Mickelson

SOLID SHOTS AND
MULLIGANS

You've hit some good shots in the decisions you've made, the relationships you've developed, and the attitudes you've embraced. You've also hit some shots you'd like to have back. That's okay; everyone does. As you go through this journal, take note of these—both the solid shots and the areas of life where you need a mulligan. Be patient and give yourself plenty of grace. Over time, you will see your need for mulligans decreasing.

SOLID SHOTS	MULLIGANS

SOLID SHOTS AND MULLIGANS

SOLID SHOTS	MULLIGANS

Solid shots	Mulligans

SOLID SHOTS AND MULLIGANS

Solid shots	Mulligans

Solid shots	Mulligans

PRAYERS
YOUR CONVERSATIONS WITH GOD

Prayer is simply mental or verbal conversation with God and his Son, Jesus. They know your heart; your life is an open book to them. They love hearing from you and want you to experience their love, forgiveness, and direction. As you read through this journal, you will likely think of situations or people you want to talk to God about—relationships in which you would like to see reconciliation and restoration, or directions you sense God is leading you to pursue. It's important not only to share your heart with God but also to listen to his soft, quiet voice as he speaks to you about your life.

Be assured that God always wants the very best for you, so seek his wisdom and insights as if his hand was on your shoulder guiding you. Learn to see people and situations the way he sees them. You may want to note the date you have these conversations or make requests, and then the date a specific prayer is answered. This is a great way to see God's hand in your life and the lives of others.

PRAYERS	DATES

The Mulligan Journal

PRAYERS	DATES

PRAYERS—YOUR CONVERSATIONS WITH GOD

PRAYERS	DATES

PRAYERS	DATES

ABOUT THE AUTHORS

Wally Armstrong is a retired professional golfer who has competed in over 320 PGA Tour events throughout the course of his career, including being a two-time runner-up and fifth in the 1978 Masters. He is a golf clinician, speaker, and the author of numerous books including the bestselling *In His Grip* with co-author Jim Sheard and *The Mulligan* with co-author Ken Blanchard. Wally lives in Maitland, Florida, with his wife, Debbie.

Ken Blanchard is an American author, leadership expert, and motivational speaker. His writing career includes more than 65 books, including *The Mulligan* and the iconic bestseller *The One Minute Manager*. Blanchard is the chief spiritual officer of The Ken Blanchard Companies, an international management training and consulting firm that he and his wife, Marjorie Blanchard, co-founded in 1979 in San Diego, California. He also cofounded Lead Like Jesus, a worldwide organization committed to helping people become servant leaders.

Chris Tiegreen is an award-winning author of more than 60 books and discussion guides, including several one-year devotionals. He has also been a journalist, pastor, and missionary, and currently teaches history at a state university. Chris is thankful for golf, even during a bad round, and lives in Atlanta with his wife, Hannah.

MORE RESOURCES

Connecting Faith & Golf – Mulligan Club

MulliganClub.org is a community where faith and golf connect. It's designed for anyone needing a "life mulligan"—receiving the Ultimate Mulligan, hearing inspiring second-chance stories, connecting to local support groups, or discovering resources offering hope and forgiveness. Find key connections and insights to enable you to get back on the fairway of mending family relationships, connecting kids to golf, finding purpose in your work, overcoming skepticism, and finding Jesus as your Caddy as you complete the course laid out before you.

Connecting Kids & Golf – Payne Stewart Kids Golf Foundation

Visit **TheMulliganMovie.com** for more information about The Mulligan movie.